Old Cottages, Farm-houses, and Other Stone Buildings in the Cotsworld District; Examples of Minor Domestic Architecture in Gloucestershire, Oxfordshire, Northants, Worcestershire [etc.] Illus. on One Hundred Collotype Plates From Photographs Specially...

OLD COTTAGES

FARM-HOUSES ETC. IN

THE COTSWOLD DISTRICT

PREFACE

THE success which attended the publication of the volume entitled "*Old Cottages and Farm Houses in Kent and Sussex*" encouraged the publisher, in fulfilment of a promise made in the Preface of that work, to follow it by the issue of similar volumes dealing with the minor domestic buildings of other counties; and it is not surprising that he should have decided to devote one of these to the delightfully characteristic work of the Cotswolds.

This district contains some of the most typical stone buildings in England, and they illustrate in a wonderful manner the methods adopted by the old builders in producing most pleasing effects by the employment of one single material. Amongst them are some of the most noteworthy houses in the country, celebrated equally from an historic and a picturesque point of view; but although these are outside the scope of this work, the smaller buildings dealt with in it show in their detail and construction the same high standard of work and design.

Year by year the public show an increasing appreciation of the artistic qualities of the domestic buildings of England, and this neighbourhood, containing some of the most beautiful examples to be found, will appeal to all lovers of the picturesque in architecture.

Mr. W. Galsworthy Davie has taken the charming series of photographs, showing the special characteristics of the Cotswold style, which although resembling in its main outlines similar work in other parts of the country, here exemplifies in the greatest possible degree the perfect adaptability of material to design.

The descriptive notes, and the illustrations accompanying them are the result of many years of personal study and knowledge of the locality, and although they do not pretend in any way to have exhausted the subject, it is hoped, they may be helpful and interesting alike to the architect and such artists and amateurs as take an interest in these matters.

E. GUY DAWBER.

22, BUCKINGHAM STREET,
   ADELPHI, LONDON,
      December, 1904.

ALPHABETICAL LIST OF PLATES

ARRANGED UNDER NAMES OF TOWNS AND VILLAGES

	Plate
ARLINGTON, Glos., Cottages at Awkward Hill	23
ASTON SUBEDGE, Glos., The Village School	50, 51
BAMPTON, Oxon., The School House	56
BARFORD, Oxon., A Farmhouse	64
BIBURY, Glos., A Cottage	24
,, ,, Groups of Cottages	70, 71
BLISWORTH, Northants., A Cottage at	22
BOURTON-ON-THE-HILL, Glos., The Baker's House	77
,, ,, The Carpenter's Shop	78
BOURTON-ON-THE-WATER, Glos., A House at	66
BROADWAY, Worc., A Cottage Window	76
,, ,, The Court Farm	52
,, ,, Top Farm	30, 31
,, ,, View in the Village Street	27
,, ,, See Laverton	
BURFORD, Oxon., House in the High Street	96
,, ,, The Tolsey	97
CALLOWELL near STROUD, Glos., The Plough Inn	62
,, ,, ,, Callowell Farm	94

LIST OF PLATES

			Plate
CAMPDEN, Glos.,	A House in the High Street	.	9
,, ,,	A Street House . .	. .	61
,, ,,	Cottages .	. .	59
,, ,,	The "Almonry" .	.	32
,, ,,	The Almshouses .	.	10
,, ,,	The Market Hall	. .	11
,, ,,	View of the Main Street	.	98
,, ,,	· See Westington		
CHALFORD HILL, near STROUD, Glos., Cottages			8, 41
CHEDWORTH, Glos., Cottages		. .	. 16, 95
,, ,,	A House	. .	91
CHURCH ICCOMB, Glos., A Cottage		.	73
CIRENCESTER, Glos., A Street View		.	46
COLN ROGER, Glos., The Rectory .		.	90
COLN ST. ALDWYN, Glos., Cottages		.	6
,, ,,	Dean Row	.	75
COLLEY WESTON, Northants, The Grocer's Shop		.	29
DUCKLINGTON, Oxon., The Post Office		.	19
DUDDINGTON, Northants, A Cottage		.	58
EBRINGTON, Glos., Cottages		.	85
FINSTOCK, Oxon., A Cottage		.	18
,, ,,	Cottages .	.	17
GRETTON, Northants., A Cottage		.	20
,, ,,	A Farmhouse	.	15
,, ,,	The Manor House .		21
HARRINGWORTH, Northants., The Swan Inn		.	12
LAVERTON, near BROADWAY, Glos., A Farmhouse		.	34, 35

LIST OF PLATES

	Plate
LAVERTON, Cottages	88
,, The Doorway, Bowmeadow Farm	43
LECHLADE, Glos., The Swan Inn	60
LEONARD STANLEY, Glos., A Farmhouse	100
LILFIELD, near STROUD, Glos., A Cottage	42
LITTLE RISSINGTON, Glos., A Cottage	3
,, A Farmhouse, Street Front	13
,, A Farmhouse, Back View	14
LYDDINGTON, Rutland, A Gable from	65
MICKLETON, Glos., Medford House, Front View	80
,, ,, ,, The Entrance	81
,, ,, ,, The East End	82
,, ,, ,, The Kitchen Chimney	83
,, ,, Tudor House	25
NASSINGTON, Northants., A Cottage	67
,, ,, A Farmhouse	63
OUNDLE, Northants., The White Lion Inn	93
PAINSWICK, Glos., A Street View	37
,, ,, Cottages	89
PAXFORD, Glos., A Farmhouse	79
RAMSDEN, Oxon., The Manor Farm	48
RISSINGTON, Glos., See Little Rissington	
SAINTBURY, Glos., A Farmhouse	36
SNOWSHILL, Glos., A House	26
STANTON, Glos., A Farmhouse	1
,, ,, Cottages	4

LIST OF PLATES

	Plate
STANTON, GLOS., COTTAGE SHOWING DORMER . .	69
,, THE VILLAGE CROSS AND A COTTAGE .	28
,, WARREN HOUSE, . . .	39
,, ,, THE DOORWAY .	40
STAMFORD, NORTHANTS., HOUSE IN ST. PAUL'S STREET .	44
,, THE BULL AND SWAN INN .	92
STANWAY, GLOS., COTTAGES	33
STOW-ON-THE-WOLD, GLOS., ST. EDWARD'S GRAMMAR SCHOOL . .	53
STROUD, GLOS. (NEAR), BACK OF INN . . .	74
,, ,, HUMPHRIES END FARM .	86
,, IN CHURCH STREET . . .	45
,, (NEAR), SEE CALLOWELL	
,, ,, SEE WOODCHESTER	
TEMPLE GUITING, GLOS., THE MANOR FARM (SOUTH FRONT) . .	54
,, THE MANOR FARM (SOUTH FRONT, END VIEW) .	55
WESTINGTON, NEAR CAMPDEN, GLOS., COTTAGES .	99
WESTON SUBEDGE, GLOS., HOUSES . . .	7, 38
,, ,, COTTAGES .	49, 68
WILLERSEY, GLOS., FARMHOUSES . . .	2, 5
,, ,, THE VILLAGE INN . .	84
WITHINGTON, GLOS., A COTTAGE . . .	47
,, ,, THE MANOR HOUSE .	72
WOODCHESTER, NEAR STROUD, GLOS., A HOUSE .	87
YARWELL, NORTHANTS., COTTAGES . . .	57

LIST OF ILLUSTRATIONS IN THE TEXT

No		Page
1.	Plan of Cottage at Iccomb, Glos.	11
2.	,, ,, Snowshill (*see* Plate xxvii)	11
3.	,, ,, Aston Subedge	12
4.	,, ,, Chedworth	13
5.	Cottage at the Cross, Stanton (*see* Plate xxviii)	14
6.	Beam in Ceiling at Broadway	15
7.	Plan of Cottage at Stanton	16
8.	Floor of Cottage at Weston Subedge	19
9.	Porch at Manor Farm, Clifton, near Deddington, Oxon.	20
10, 11.	Details of Porch at Manor Farm, Clifton	21
12, 13.	Doors at Iccomb, Glos.	22
14.	Doorway at Aston Subedge	23
15.	,,. Broadway, Worc.	23
16, 17.	,, Gretton, Northants, with details	24
18.	,, Gretton, Northants.	24
19.	Doorhead at Campden	25
20.	,, Stow-on-the-Wold	25
21.	,, Campden	25
22.	Door at Bourton-on-the-Water	26
23.	Doorheads at Chipping Campden	26
24, 25, 26, 27.	Casement Fastenings and Hinge from Broadway and other Places	27
28.	Window and details, St. Edward's School, Stow-on-the-Wold	29

xii LIST OF ILLUSTRATIONS IN THE TEXT

No		Page
29.	Window at Gretton, Northants.	32
30.	Typical Hollow " Perpendicular " Label	33
31, 32, 33.	Mouldings from the Almshouses, Campden	33
34.	Window and details at Wansford, Northants.	34
35.	Window at Iccomb	35
36.	Lead-Glazing from Broadway	36
37.	,, ,, Tewkesbury	36
38.	An Oval Window from Mickleton	36
39.	Ventilator from a House near Campden	36
40.	A Gable in St. Paul's Street, Stamford	38
41.	Panel from the Gable at Stamford, shown on Fig. 40	39
42	Gable Opening, Top Farm, Broadway	39
43.	,, ,, At Stanton	39
44.	Date Tablet at Gretton, Northants	40
45.	,, ,, at Spratton, Northants	40
46.	,, ,, at East Haddon, Northants.	40
47.	,, ,, at the Manor House, Gretton	40
48	,, ,, at Chipping Campden	40
49.	,, ,, at Stanton (*see* Plate i)	40
50.	Plan of House at Aston Subedge (now the Village School)	42
51.	Doorway of the Village School, Aston Subedge	43
52.	Chimney Stacks at Broadway	43
53.	Cap of a Broadway Chimney	44
54.	Chimney Cap at Stanton	44
55.	,, ,, at Burford	44
56.	Typical Profiles of Chimney Cornices	44
57.	Chimney from Kingham	45
58.	,, on a Barn at Bredon, Worc.	45
59.	,, from Bibury	45
60, 61.	Method of forming Ridge Cresting	48
62.	A Dovecote at Bibury	49

LIST OF ILLUSTRATIONS IN THE TEXT

No.		Page
63.	Pigeon-holes in a wall, Stow-on-the-Wold	50
64.	Finial at Weston Subedge	52
65.	Finial of Gable at Top Farm, Broadway	52
66.	Gothic Finial on a Barn at Longborough	52
67.	Finial at Campden	52
68.	„ from Chastleton	52
69.	„ „ Broadway	52
70.	„ „ „	53
71.	Typical Forms of Gable Copings	53
72.	Gable Termination from Snowshill	54
73.	„ „ „ Winchcombe	54
74.	Kneeler from Deddington, Oxon.	54
75.	„ „ Gretton, Northants.	54
76.	„ „ Broadwell	55
77.	Plaster Patterns formerly on a House at Stow-on-the-Wold	56
78.	Stone Chimney-piece, Manor House, Turkdean, dated 1588	57
79.	Fireplace at Darlingscott	58
80.	Plan of Medford House, Mickleton	59
81.	Entrance Pier at Medford House, Mickleton	60
82.	Archway Entrance at Burford	61
83.	Oriel Window at Burford	62
84.	Coat of Arms on the Market Hall, Chipping Campden	68
85.	String at the " Kite's Nest," Campden	68
86.	A Gable at Campden	70

Old Cottages, Farm-houses, etc., in the Cotswold District

AMONGST the Cotswold hills are to be found examples of domestic architecture, as characteristic as in any other part of England, and although perhaps they do not rank in importance with larger or more pretentious edifices, they possess a singular interest and quiet charm of their own.

The cottages, like the manor houses, the churches and farm-buildings, are all built of the native stone, and all are gabled and picturesque. Perhaps nowhere is there any architecture more perfect in its simplicity and grace than that found in these old English villages.

The houses and hamlets form a more or less distinctive group, and are of great value as showing how simple and truthful building, in the hands of rustic craftsmen and designers, without outside influence, may develop an almost traditional style.

Just as the various phases of architecture have been classified into so-called periods, so with this essentially local type of the Cotswolds, which is in reality a product of evolution, growing out of the inherited knowledge of the wants which the builders had to satisfy, and of the natural material at their disposal. In the Middle Ages, and down to the eighteenth century, architecture, or building, as it is better called, was always influenced by local conditions, and the character of work was much the same all over the country; while such cosmopolitan methods as we adopt to-day were quite unknown.

From the earliest days the Cotswold hills were notable as pasture for sheep, which roamed the downs that spread in almost unbroken succession from the Severn to the Thames. As far back as the twelfth century wool was one of our staple articles of export, being sold to Italy and Flanders.

English wool, and that from the Cotswold districts in particular, was esteemed beyond any other, and before we began the manufacture of woollen goods, we exported so much unwrought wool, that the breeding and feeding of sheep was the general occupation, and it is owing to this that many towns and villages, long since fallen to decay, were once prosperous and wealthy.

This prosperity led to the great era of church building throughout Gloucestershire and Northamptonshire, when so many noble buildings, such as Northleach, Cirencester, Burford, etc., were erected by the pious munificence of the wealthy merchants of the staple. It also brought fortunes to the local "Woolmen," as they were called, and an excellent subsistence to hundreds of their workpeople; indeed, it is not too much to say that it is due to their large trade in wool that the small towns and villages, scattered about these hills, are so full of finely built and beautiful houses.

Centuries ago the Cotswolds were one great sheep-walk from end to end, and what with the wool from his sheep, and the grain from his fields, the Cotswold farmer was well-to-do. But now, alas! those times are no more, and the great barns stand empty, or are allowed to fall into ruins; but they speak very

IN THE COTSWOLD DISTRICT

eloquently of the days when this district was one of the wealthiest and most prosperous in all England.

The country at first sight seems wild and bare. The great stretches of upland, chill and oppress the casual visitor with a sense of loneliness and melancholy, and perhaps it is only those who live day by day amongst its rolling hills that appreciate and love its beauties, for the Cotswolds possess a distinctive character of their own, and are unlike any other part of England. The richness of the colour of the soil, the depth of tone in the foliage, and the wonderful deep purples and blues of the hills, all combine to make pictures that appeal to all lovers of English rural scenery.

Geologically these hills form a portion of the great belt of limestones, which extends across England from the Dorsetshire coast to between Filey and Scarborough. To architects in particular the whole formation is of unusual interest, as within these limits are found almost all the building limestones used in England. The hills form an elevated tableland or plateau some 800 to 1,200 feet above sea level, with a fairly steep escarpment facing west, and overlooking the valley of the Severn. This escarpment was perhaps a cliff range overhanging an arm of the sea, but the tableland behind has been cut into valleys by frost, rain, and streams, and swept completely bare of the gravels which lie so thick in the valleys beneath.

The various strata which dip slightly to the S.E. and E., comprise the whole of the Oolite series, a vast mass of more or less continuous beds of limestone, separated by partings of clay. These are all of marine origin and enclose, in places, great amounts of shelly matter; such as beds of oysters, and reefs of coral. The series begins with the Inferior Oolitic limestones, which stretch from Bridport northward to Beaminster and Sherborne, and broaden out on to the flat-topped Cotswold hills east of Cheltenham. These are succeeded by a band of the clayey substance known as Fuller's earth, which, forming a water-bearing zone amongst the hills, supplies the numerous springs found on all sides.

The great or Bath Oolite has at its base the well-known Stonesfield slate, which splits into the coarse fissile slabs, commonly used for roofing. The middle and lower beds give the best stone for building purposes; soft when first quarried, but possessing the well-known property of hardening with exposure.

The stone is usually quarried from about April to October, after which the quarries are closed for the winter months. It is generally obtained by clearing away the upper layers of inferior stone and loose brash, though sometimes it is mined for, as most of the Bath stones are. When first quarried it is rather yellow in tone, but becomes bleached by exposure, and after a time turns to all manner of rich colours, and is quickly covered with lichens, for which it seems to have a peculiar attraction. It is an admirable weather stone, as much old work in the district testifies.

Nearly every village at one time had its local quarry, though many of these have for years been unworked, and it is doubtless owing to their proximity to excellent stone, and the ease with which it could be obtained, that the larger towns like Painswick, Northleach, Burford, Campden and many others grew so rapidly and prospered. Much of the stone used in building St. Paul's Cathedral came from quarries close to Burford, and in that church there is a marble tablet to the memory of Christopher Kempster, who was employed as master mason. These quarries, still called Christopher's or Kitt's quarries, lie a little to the south-west of Burford, and near to them is a large stone house bearing the inscription, " Christopher Kempster built this in 1698."

Owing to the nature of the formation of the hills, the whole district is essentially a stone one, and all the buildings are constructed of the local limestone, which lies everywhere within a few feet of the surface. It is doubtless to this, together with the isolated positions of the villages and hamlets, cut off in many cases from the main arteries of traffic, that we owe their preservation to-day, and as stone was practically the only material available, we cannot but admire the ingenious way in which the old builders adapted it in their work.

Generally speaking we do not in this district find much domestic work of an earlier date than the close of the sixteenth century, and the bulk of the essentially traditional Cotswold style ranges from that time to 1700. Perhaps this may be attributed to the fact that during this period there were more resident gentry in the country than at any other, and they depended more or less for their livelihood on the produce of their estates. They therefore encouraged building, both amongst themselves and the tenants and inhabitants of their properties, and did much to influence the taste of the time.

During the reign of Queen Anne, when the commercial classes became such a power in the country, owing to the great expansion of English trade, and fortunes were quickly made, many of the old Royalist families, who had suffered first by the Civil War, and then by the reckless extravagance of the Restoration, were forced to sell their estates. The wealthy merchants bought them up and expended money in either building new houses for themselves, or in adding to and altering the old ones, but though this latter phase of work is particularly interesting, it stands in a category by itself, and cannot be called so essentially a Cotswold style as that of the seventeenth century.

It is doubtful too whether these people, having no ancestral interest in their purchases, did not somewhat neglect the village social life, for during the eighteenth century and even in later years, when the labouring classes became very poor, it was no uncommon occurrence for them to be turned out of their villages, and their cottages pulled down, so that they should not become a burden on the landowners. This in a great measure accounts for the lack of cottage building between the end of the seventeenth century and the middle of the nineteenth.

Broadly speaking the recognized Cotswold type belongs to the period between 1580 and 1690. It was a thoroughly commonsense style of building, based on tradition handed down through generations of village craftsmen, and it remained without change for nearly a century. The main bulk of the buildings were without doubt erected by local men, and without any external aid, for we find the same methods adopted, with but slight local variations, many miles apart. It was a style that was gradually evolved: at first retaining a few links with the so-called Perpendicular work of the preceding century, but slowly shaking these off, until in the course of some few years it settled down to be the traditional work of the day, the vernacular of building in which the craftsman expressed his ideas.

It is no idle plea to urge that this phase of English domestic architecture, although of a humbler sort, merits as much attention and careful study as that of our larger houses and ecclesiastical buildings, for these cottages were built to be lived in by the dwellers of these country villages, and belong to a type of house-building and craftsmanship quite unknown to us to-day.

Occasionally the individuality of the craftsman shows itself in the way of quaint finials, or some delicate wrought iron work to the doors or windows; small touches that give a charm and vitality to his work.

In these cosmopolitan days the use of railways and cheap means of transit have almost obliterated the older crafts, and the advent of bricks and mortar, corrugated iron and foreign timber, is very rapidly driving the local materials and methods of building out of use. This cannot be sufficiently deplored, for apart from its effect upon the employment of labour, it is a matter of serious import that the old handicrafts, which made this country so pre-eminently beautiful, are dying out. The total lack of encouragement given to workers in these simple trades, and the introduction of methods of building quite at variance with those indigenous to the country, combined with the enforcement of restrictive Building Byelaws, are bound in the course of a few years to have a disastrous effect, even if they have not done so already.

In the districts with which we are dealing, it is now a somewhat rare occurrence to find new cottages built with local materials; if they are so it is chiefly by people who have at heart the old traditions, and therefore resist new and strange innovations.

This beautiful type of building, so simple and so strong, and which is as worthy of retention and preservation as any other either in this country or abroad, has never been appreciated at its real value, and buildings both great and small are either allowed to fall into a state of hopeless ruin, or, which is almost worse, to suffer such " restoration " as to render them quite unrecognizable.

Of course we must recollect that the builders of these houses had none of the difficulties to contend with that are ever present to-day. Drainage and sanitation were practically unknown in the way we understand them; water supply and the consequent introduction of pipes inside the house, together with the complication of modern requirements and the over elaboration of planning, were non-existent, so that, when examined in detail they are found to be simple both in plan and arrangement. The absence of small outbuildings, which detract from the restfulness of the main house, all contributed towards the desired effect, as in the farmhouse at Willersey, illustrated on Plate v.

More than anything else the sense of proportion in these houses is the one thing that produces so much of their charm. It is always correct, there is never a false note, for these old builders seem to have understood intuitively the exact relation of voids and solids, of heights and widths, and in a quiet and unpretentious way their houses are almost perfect as specimens of village craftsmanship and building. An admirable example of this type is shown in the Rectory at Coln Roger (Plate xc).

There was no striving after any eccentricities or unnecessary embellishment; what was good enough for their fathers was good enough for them, and there are villages with houses dating and ranging from the end of the sixteenth to well into the eighteenth century precisely similar in detail, showing how thoroughly these people were imbued with one idea of building.

It may be thought that these villages and country towns are all of a stereotyped pattern and somewhat monotonous, but nothing could be farther from this in reality, as a glance through the illustrations will show, for though there is a repetition of certain forms and features, and we recognize at once that every detail is familiar, yet it is this very similarity of idea permeating the whole of the district during this period that gives such a broad and dignified character to the work (compare for example Plates xxx and lxxii).

The houses were mostly placed in such positions as would

IN THE COTSWOLD DISTRICT

shelter them from exposure to the weather, and give ready access to such roads as then existed. This however was by no means always the case. Apparently no attention was paid to the question of aspect, as to whether the position commanded good views— indeed many of the sites seem particularly ill chosen, lying low, or close to streams, but this last point, in the case of the houses in the Painswick and Stroud valleys, was necessary for the carrying on of trade. Some illustrations of this type are given on Plates lxxiv, lxxxvii and xc.

It is a mistake to suppose, as many people do, that the work of these old time builders was always sound and constructional, and to hold it up as an example to us of to-day, for although they built according to their idea of what was truthful, much of what they did we must perforce condemn now.

Their walls, for instance, though thick and solid in appearance, were often merely an inner and outer shell, filled with rubbish and small stones, which had little or no cohesive properties and consequently could not withstand any settlements, and suffered severely from the effects of wet and frost.

Many of the houses were erected without any foundations, and in some cases the builders never even troubled to remove the turf, but began their walls directly from the surface of the ground.

An eaves gutter, or downspout to carry off the rain was absolutely unknown in a Cotswold house, and the water running directly off the roof, was either blown against the walls, or dripped to the ground, thus accounting for the decayed and worn condition of the base of the walls.

In some of the houses having an occasional parapet and lead gutter, the water emptied itself through a stone gurgoyle, projecting some two or three feet from the wall, a system nearly as bad as the former one, for instead of the water being distributed evenly around the house, it was here collected into a larger volume, which perhaps did greater damage to the building.

The use of lead for any purpose, except window glazing, was in these smaller houses evidently unknown, as a lead head or downspout is never found except in large and important buildings. The wooden V-shaped eaves gutter, and square down pipes, were first used when the necessity became apparent for some means of getting rid of the water, and it is only during the last century that these have been superseded by the iron ones now more or less universal.

No doubt a great deal of the charm of these old houses is due to the fact that they were nearly always self-contained. An admirable example is shown in the cottage by the Cross at Stanton (Plate xxviii). The eaves projected without any gutters or spouting, the breadth of wall surface was unbroken by the vertical lines of down pipes, which cut all modern buildings into strips, and such things as ventilation pipes and sanitary monstrosities being then unknown.

When the houses were built on sloping sites advantage was nearly always taken of it, to cleverly arrange some of the rooms on a lower level and by means of terraces and steps add to the picturesque appearance of the buildings—but unfortunately these lower rooms, owing to wet and damp, are now almost unusable except as store places (*see* Plates xvi, xxvii, xciv).

As the rooms had outer walls on each side, on the ground floors particularly, and windows in them, they were always cheerful and sunny, but with regard to the bedrooms it was different.

At this period—the seventeenth century—it was for some strange reason thought injurious to sleep in rooms facing the sun, so most of the original rooms faced north and east, opening off a passage, or else out of each other.

IN THE COTSWOLD DISTRICT

The stairs generally ascended in the middle of the house, direct into a room and, as Mr. Baring Gould says in his "*Old Country Life*," "At the head of the stairs slept the master and his wife, and all the rooms tenanted by the rest of the household were accessible only through that. The daughters of the house and maidservants lay in rooms on one side, say the right, with the maids in those most distant; those of the men lay on the left, the sons of the house nearest the chamber of the master and the serving men furthest off."

This arrangement of rooms opening out of each other, on a

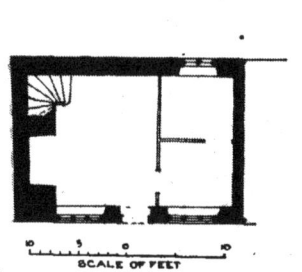
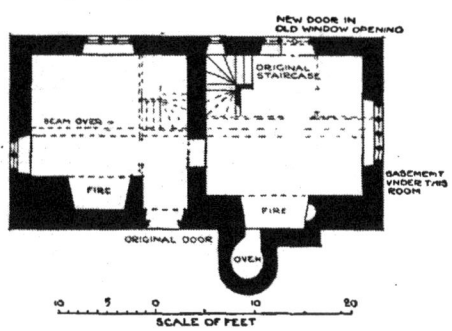

FIG. 1. PLAN OF COTTAGE AT ICCOMB, GLOS.

FIG. 2. PLAN OF COTTAGE AT SNOWSHILL (*see* also Plate xxvii).

somewhat simplified scale, is frequently met with to-day, though as a rule an additional staircase gives access to the servants' quarters, from the kitchen below, but the great length of many of the houses shows that the custom must have been universal, as illustrated in Plates v and l.

If we look at the plans of any of these small houses, the first thing that strikes us is the absolute simplicity, not to say baldness, of their arrangement (*see* Figs. 1, 2, 3). The bulk of them have now been converted into two or more separate dwellings, and though many of the later alterations appear at a first glance to have entirely changed the original plan, it is quite easy to reconstruct it. As single houses they consisted of two or three rooms on the ground floor, one, perhaps the living room, being rather larger than the others (*see* Figs. 1, 2, 3). In arrangement these houses carried on the mediæval tradition of the one general living and sleeping room, with the "solar" opening off it, for beyond the actual rooms themselves there was nothing; no store cupboards, larders, or conveniences of any description, and everything was contained within the four outer walls.

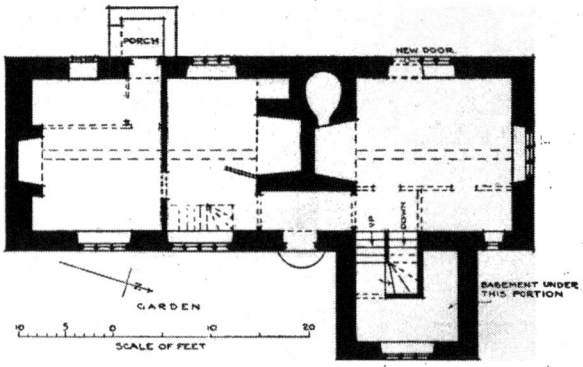

FIG. 3. PLAN OF COTTAGE AT ASTON SUBEDGE.

They were always planned one room in thickness, (*see* Fig. 4), so that they could be roofed in a single span, and the invariable width is from 16 to 18 feet. When more accommodation was needed, they were made L, E, or H shaped, with a central block and projecting wings, but however large the house, always retaining the single span roof.

Another characteristic, noticeable in each room, is the large fireplace, which gives a greater suggestion of comfort and warmth than almost any other structural feature. It was the spot around which the family would cluster after the day's work in the fields or at the loom, was done, and where the meals were cooked. Most of these fireplaces are very large, as a comparison with the plans will show—frequently 6 feet and upwards in width (*see* Figs. 3 and 4). They were not high—about 4 to 5 feet being the average, and the head was either formed of large stones, shaped as a flat four centred arch, or spanned with a plain lintol of oak. Wood was the usual fuel, burnt on the stone hearth, and pots and kettles were hung from the iron hinged trivet, fixed in one of the innermost angles.

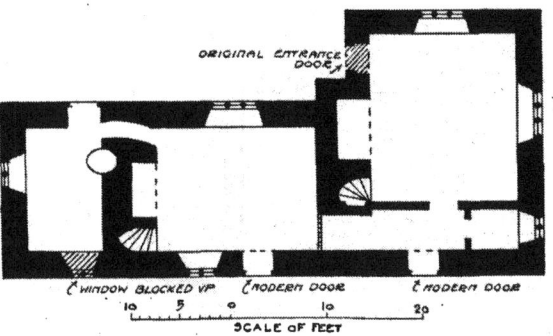

FIG. 4. PLAN OF COTTAGE AT CHEDWORTH.

Sometimes we find the flat iron ovens standing on the stone hearth, and on the top of these the fire is laid. These ovens are about 2 feet square and 7 or 8 inches deep, placed between small projecting stone piers, with moulded caps, and between these again is the iron fireback. These latter are found in many old houses doubtless owing to their proximity to the coal and iron fields of the Forest of Dean, but few have any great merit, unless it be that of plainness, and none show the exquisite workmanship of the Kent and Sussex examples. The bread oven, in which the faggots were burned, generally opened out of one side of the fireplace, and was sometimes built in the thickness of the wall, or else jutting out in the form of a semicircle with a small roof over it as in the house at Snowshill (*see* Fig. 4 and Plate xxvi). On one or both sides of the fireplace, inside the ingle, a seat was often arranged, in the thickness of the masonry. This consisted of a hollowed out recess, with a stone or wooden bottom, just wide enough for a person to sit down in comfortably, and arched above the head. Some few inches up on each side there were small places hollowed out to take the elbows, or else to stand a glass or cup upon, as in the cottage at Stanton (*see* Fig. 5). Sometimes little cupboards were fitted in on either side of the fireplace as receptacles for food, or pipes and tobacco, as at Medford house (*see* Fig. 80), and occasionally we find small windows behind the seats to light the ingle, but as a rule there are none.

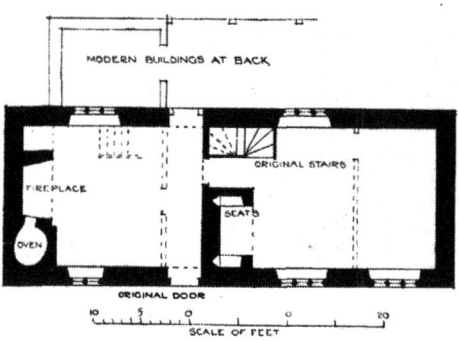

FIG. 5. COTTAGE AT THE CROSS, STANTON.

Though their close proximity to the fire has its drawbacks, yet these warm seats are much coveted corners, and in the village inns to-day one frequently sees the old labourers putting up willingly with smarting eyes and general discomfort rather than shift their places.

When these houses were built reading was not much in vogue, and light was not wanted for that purpose. The women of the household evidently did not use the chimney corners for sewing in, owing to the smoke, and doubtless they were chiefly occupied by the men and children. These old ingle nooks, the real genuine article, usually have a large tapering flue carried straight up and open to the sky above. They doubtless smoked exceedingly, as the blackened ceilings show, but as doors and windows fitted badly and draughts must have been abundant, a little smoke more or less could have been of no great consequence!

With the exception of the internal fireplaces and chimney-breasts it is seldom that the rooms are divided by stone walls; the partitions were generally made of strong oak framing, filled in with lath and plaster, or panelled with oak.

The smaller buildings therefore, unless the chimney stack happened to be inside the house, had practically no lateral tie, and this is one of the reasons why so many houses are found with their walls out of plumb, the weight of the roof having thrust them out of the perpendicular.

The floors were carried on joists from wall to wall, or more frequently resting on beams, placed centrally in the rooms without any regard to the positions of the windows and fireplaces, over which they happened to come.

These floors, in the cottages, were generally of unsquared joists of timber, often with the bark left on, laid some few inches apart and packed in between with a mixture of clay and chopped straw on interlacing hazel sticks. Underneath the ceiling was plastered, with the floor above either laid with oak boards or else finished with a smooth cement face. Sometimes in the better class houses, the joists were squared and moulded, as at Broadway (Fig. 6), and showed as an open ceiling below.

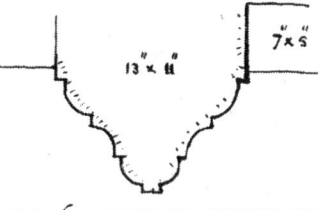

FIG. 6.   BEAM IN CEILING AT BROADWAY.

In the smaller houses it will be seen that the ground floor

rooms are very much alike in size (*see* Fig. 7). In the seventeenth and eighteenth centuries, spinning and weaving formed one of the occupations of many of the inhabitants. The spinning wheel converted the wool into worsted, which again was woven into cloth; this of course was some years before the great mills in the Stroud valley monopolized the bulk of the industry.

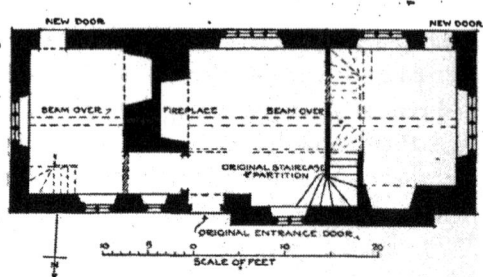

FIG. 7. PLAN OF COTTAGE AT STANTON.

The hand-looms have long since disappeared, but the spinning wheels are even now sometimes found amongst the forgotten lumber of the oldest houses, and in the villages around Campden there still exist a few old people who can call to mind hand-looms being used in the cottages.

The walls of the houses which are always of stone throughout, are never less than 18 inches, and often considerably more than 2 feet in thickness. They are composed of rubble stone laid in rather thin layers, or in thicker courses of roughly dressed ashlar, the character of the walling depending in a great measure on the way in which the stone comes from the quarry. Where the stone is only obtained in large blocks the walling is built either of roughly-squared pieces, with regular coursed joints, as in the illustration of the farmhouse at Stanton, (Plate i), or at Laverton, (Plate xxxiv), or else the window dressings and angle quoins are of pieces of dressed stone and the general walling built of random rubble as in the grocer's shop at Colley Weston, (Plate xxix), or of coursed rubble as shown in the illustration of the farmhouse, at Gretton,

(Plate xv), and the cottages at Bibury (Plate lxx). It is therefore easy to tell at a glance from the character of the walling the nature of the stone found in the local quarries.

In many cases in the better class work, this ashlar is carefully dressed and laid square on the beds and upright joints, as in the illustration of the almshouses and market hall at Campden, (Plates x and xi), but this was a costly method of building and is not often met with in the smaller houses.

In the districts where the stone is not found in block, but comes out in thin layers of from 2 to 6 inches thick, the type of walling is again quite different, for here the stone is laid in courses almost as it comes from the quarry, on its natural bed, and the only dressed stone that is used is that to the angles and around the doors and windows—as seen in the illustrations at Harringworth in Northants, (Plate xii), and Little Rissington and Chedworth in Gloucestershire (Plate xvi).

In many cases, especially in the eighteenth century, when wooden windows came into use, the ordinary walling stone was built around them, without any dressings at all—as in the illustrations from Finstock (Plate xvii) and Ducklington (Plate xix) in Oxfordshire.

In quite unpretentious buildings the stone was built in the walls, without any attempt to dress the face, beyond knocking off the projections with the hammer as the stones were laid, and the angle quoins were roughly dressed or scabbled with the mason's axe.

In Northamptonshire we find a pleasant variety in the treatment of the walling, where alternate layers of red ironstone are interspersed with the limestone, as in Plates xx, xxi and xxii. This ironstone is found in its greatest thickness in the neighbourhood of Northampton, and is quarried largely at Duston, Blisworth, etc.

Where the stone was got out of large blocks, it had either to be axed square on the face and the beds, or else carefully dressed with the chisel, but in whatever manner worked it was always laid with wide and generous mortar joints.

In many of the old barns and farm buildings, the walling was often laid dry, without any mortar, a method that is still adhered to in field walls and farm buildings.

These dry stone walls are models of ingenious construction, for incredible as it may seem, it is almost impossible to pull out the smallest stone of a well-built wall, the stones being so admirably fitted and dovetailed together. Numerous illustrations are shown of these walls in the plates, those at Bibury and Arlington being particularly noticeable (Plates xxiii and xxiv).

The wall surface, when not left with the quarry face, and the ashlar work for the quoins and dressings, being usually coarsely cut with the chisel, no attempt being made to rub or smooth it. It is to this as much as to anything else that the walls of these buildings owe so much of their charm, for one feels that these old masons, who worked the stone, thoroughly understood their material, and, unconsciously perhaps, obtained the best value out of it in every way.

The ground floor, when there were no cellars underneath, was made of large slabs of stone, laid directly on the earth, with the result that the moisture readily soaked through, doubtless causing the rooms to be wet and unhealthy, and as damp courses were unknown when these houses were built the lower part of the walls in winter time was moist and damp. This method of laying the floors was but a slight advance on that of some century earlier, when the natural earth well trampled upon formed the only flooring. In winter, dry rushes and in summer sweet-scented herbs were spread, but even then they must have been damp and dirty, and some idea of their state may be gathered from the fact that the doorway of the hall at Winchester was widened to admit of carts coming in. This was probably the origin of the raised dais we find in so many of the old halls, and which were evidently to enable the head of the house to sit with some degree of comfort, raised above the floor, which added to his dignity and gave him a good view of his retainers.

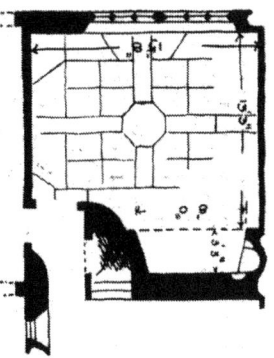

FIG. 8. FLOOR OF COTTAGE AT WESTON SUBEDGE.

In many cases the stones were laid to a pattern, as in the house at Weston Subedge, (*see* Fig. 8), where they roughly radiate from an octagonal centre, or as at Stanton where the paving of the hall is made of alternate squares of blue lias and the local limestone. In numerous cases the floors were laid according to the whim or ingenuity of the mason. The old millstone set as a front doorstep is a very frequent sight in these Cotswold villages, as shown in Plate xli.

The staircase always opened directly out of one or other of the living rooms, and is generally found by the fireplace, contained in as small a place as possible, *see* plans, (*see* Figs. 1 to 8 inclusive). It was frequently circular in plan and in many of the oldest houses was of stone, with a central newel similar to those in church towers; another instance of the manner in which old traditions lingered in these remote districts. Oak was the other material used, with a series of winders round a centre post, generally cramped and awkward to get up and down.

It is noteworthy that in all these houses the staircase, even in

FIG. 9. PORCH AT MANOR FARM, CLIFTON, NEAR DEDDINGTON, OXON.

those of the better class, was treated solely for the purpose of utility, and was but seldom made a decorative feature, for one finds houses with rooms beautifully panelled from floor to ceiling, with fine stone chimney-pieces, yet possessing staircases with no detail worthy of notice, and in no way corresponding with the rest of the building. Some of these staircases were in semi-circular turrets projecting from the main walls, finished at the top with a conical stone slated roof. At Burford there are still a few examples left, while one very fine specimen which was at the back of the *Bear Inn* has only recently been pulled down.

Another point to be noticed is the absence of any porches, no shelter being given to the door, beyond an occasional hood, or slight projection of stone, (*see* Plates xli and xlii), and these are nearly always of later date.

In the larger houses stone porches are met with, sometimes carried up two or more storeys, and finishing in a gable, but a glance through the illustrations will show that the porches at Rissington, (Plate iii), and Mickleton, (Plate xxv), are almost isolated examples if we except those at the Manor Farms at

IN THE COTSWOLD DISTRICT

Ramsden, (Plate xlviii), and Clifton in Oxfordshire, (*see* Figs. 9, 10, 11), where the regular early open type is adhered to, the latter having a moulded impost at the springing of the arch.

The smaller two-roomed houses generally had but one outer door, as in the plans of those at Snowshill and Stanton, (Figs. 4 and 5), but as they grew in size and importance, two and sometimes three outer doors are not unusual, and it is only since these houses have been cut up into separate cottages that other doors and

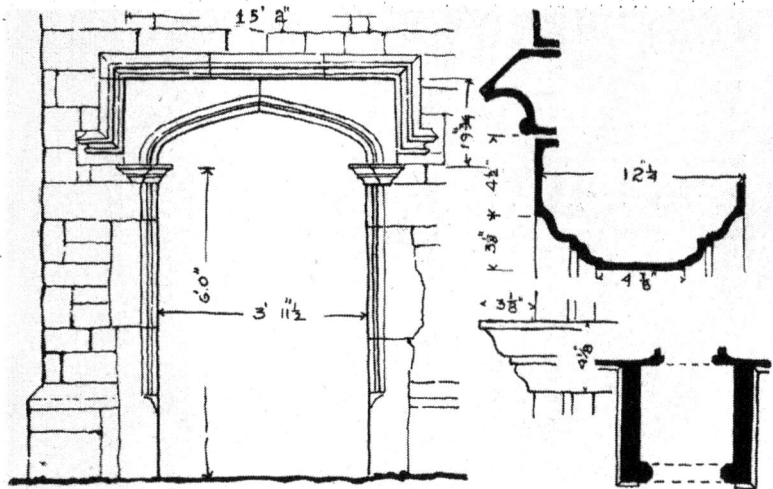

FIGS. 10, 11. PORCH AT MANOR FARM, CLIFTON.

windows have been inserted, such as were never found in the original buildings (*see* Fig. 2).

During the whole of the seventeenth century the employment of the lintol was universal, and one is struck by the almost entire absence of the arch in these buildings.

Externally the openings were never made wider than the stone would carry, and stout oak beams were used across the door and window openings inside.

22　OLD COTTAGES, FARM-HOUSES, &c.

The four-centred doorhead out of one stone is the commonest treatment. At first steep in outline, as at Colley Weston, (Plate xxix), Broadway and Campden (Plates xxxi, xxxii and xxxiii), and Stanway in Gloucestershire, it was later very generally flat, as in the numerous illustrations given.

The earlier doorways retained the label over the top, returning down on either side of the stone head, as in the farm-houses at Laverton and Saintbury, near Broadway, (Plates xxxv, xxxvi), and Painswick, (Plate xxxvii), or else treated with a simple cornice

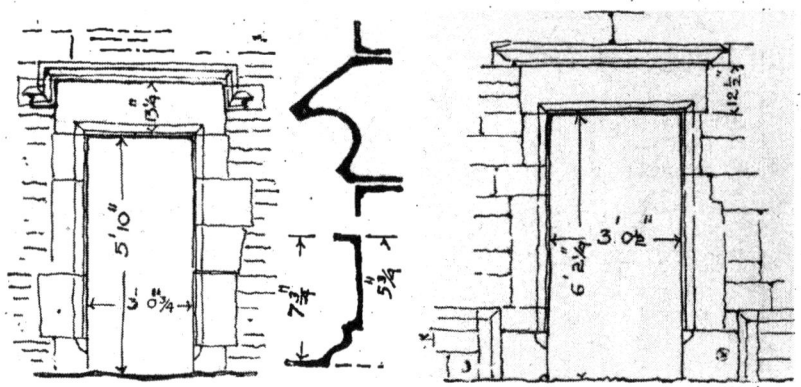

FIGS. 12, 13. DOORS AT ICCOMB, GLOS.

above the opening as at Weston Subedge and Paxford (Plates xxxviii and lxxix).

In Broadway and two or three villages adjoining, are a series of very interesting doorways, evidently executed by the same hand. The villages are only some two or three miles apart, and they were undoubtedly all carried out within a few years of each other (*see* Figs. 14 and 15). There is a strong Gothic feeling about the shape of the head, the carved spandrils, and the termination of the labels, but the detail of the mouldings, the late character of the carving, and the peculiarity of the stop to the jambs, all show evidence of the classical feeling that was at last pervading even these out of the way districts.

In one of the ends of the label in the village school at Aston Subedge the date 1663 is cut, and on the other the initials of the builder or owner (*see* Plate li and Fig. 14).

FIG. 14.
DOORWAY AT ASTON SUBEDGE.

FIG. 15.
DOORWAY AT BROADWAY, WORC.

Another interesting doorway is that from the Warren House at Stanton (Plate xl). Here we have a similar shaped head; moulded jambs, and the peculiar stops and rosettes in the spandrils, but instead of the label there is quite a classical treatment of architrave, frieze and cornice, all crudely detailed, but showing how, in the doorways, the builders were attempting some fresh treatment in place of the old traditional types

24   OLD COTTAGES, FARM-HOUSES, &c.

In some cases, as in the Northamptonshire examples, the doors had a plain straight lintol, generally treated with a fine series of mouldings, returning down the jambs, but without any label or

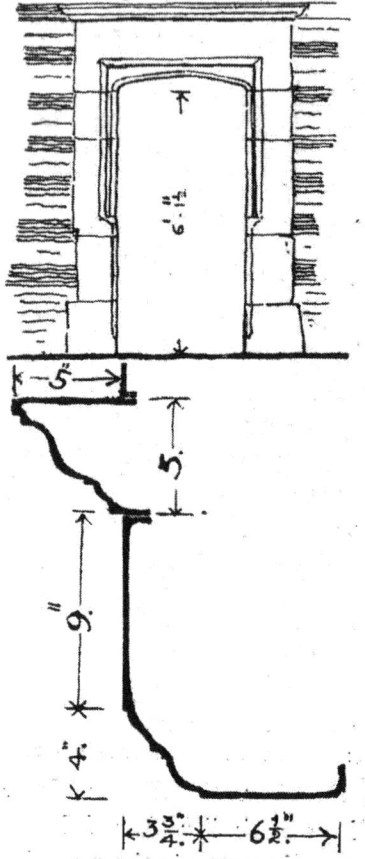

FIGS. 16, 17. DOORWAY AT GRETTON, NORTHANTS, WITH DETAILS.

FIG. 18.   A DOORWAY AT GRETTON, NORTHANTS.

cornice over, as at Gretton in Northamptonshire (*see* Fig. 18).

Occasionally the doorways were sheltered with a projecting stone hood, on moulded brackets, as at Chalford Hill near Stroud and Lechlade, (Plates xli and lx), and in Campden and Stow-on-the-Wold there is series in wood and stone of delightful and

IN THE COTSWOLD DISTRICT

pleasing variety (*see* Figs. 19 to 21).

The doorway at Bow meadow Farm, in Laverton, (Plate xliii), is a typical Cotswold example, showing all the simple charm of the style. The deep head and large stones forming the sides all impart a sense of dignity and repose to the opening, which sets off to advantage the plain oak door.

A pleasant variation of the flat four-centred head was obtained by inserting a key and impost stones, sometimes plain as at Bourton-on-the-Water, (*see* Fig. 19), and occasionally with the latter moulded as at Deddington.

The doorway has always been the centre of attraction and that upon which the best workmanship is most often found, for if there be

FIG. 19. DOORHEAD AT CAMPDEN.

FIG. 20. DOORHEAD AT STOW-ON-THE-WOLD.

FIG. 21. DOORHEAD AT CAMPDEN.

no ornament anywhere else, it is generally here that some effort was made in that direction, as we have seen in the examples referred to.

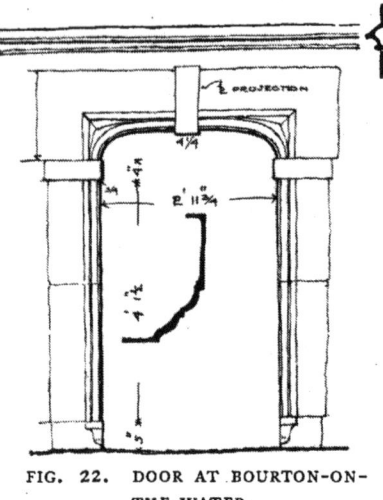

FIG. 22. DOOR AT BOURTON-ON-THE-WATER.

It must be noted that it was in doorways, fireplaces, and the memorial tombs in the churches, that the classical influence first appeared, for it was on these features that the builders generally tried to exercise their ingenuity.

The proportion of the doorway greatly affected its decoration; a wide and low opening conveying a sense of homeliness and comfort that is seldom obtained by a tall and narrow one. And in these stone houses it was the key or focus upon which their energies were concentrated, and care and thought expended (*see* Fig. 23.)

It was in the details and furnishing of their doorways, especially the external ones, that these old Cotswold builders so excelled, for the wrought iron work, the latches

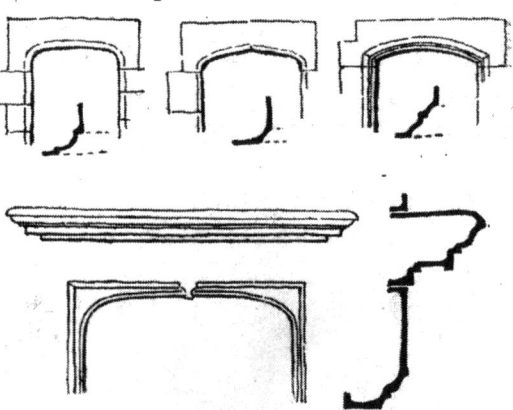

FIG. 23. DOORHEADS AT CHIPPING CAMPDEN.

IN THE COTSWOLD DISTRICT

and hinges, made and designed by the village smith, are full of charm and character. Every touch shows the delight they took in their work, and how admirably suited it was to its place.

The construction of the doors—at first upright planks nailed to cross-pieces behind, allowed for the display of the beautiful hinges and fastenings still to be seen on some old examples.

The modern method of hanging doors with what are technically called "butts" is of course responsible for the loss of much beauty, for the old way of hook and band hinges, beautifully hammered and worked, added much to the general effect of the door —it provided a good opportunity for a fine piece of design on a plain oaken background; the iron work being delicately fashioned into minute tendrils and interlacing ornament, or simply forged into strong and sturdy bands.

The handles were often

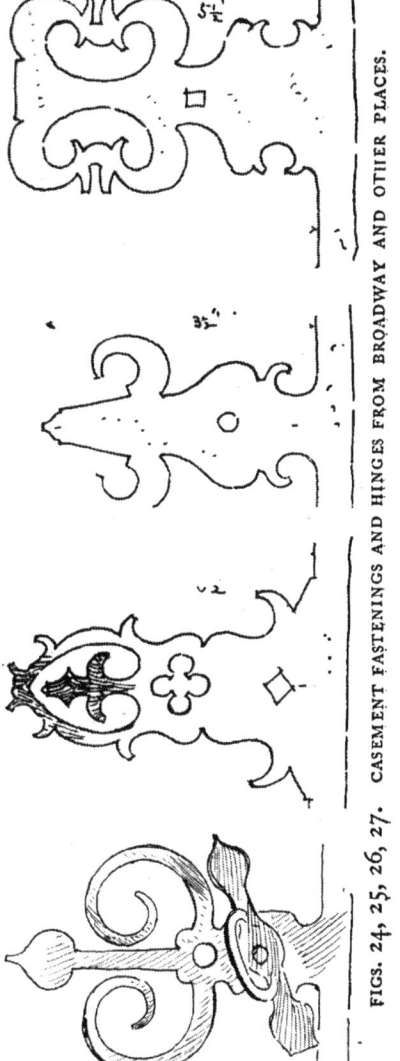

FIGS. 24, 25, 26, 27. CASEMENT FASTENINGS AND HINGES FROM BROADWAY AND OTHER PLACES.

superb pieces of craftsmanship, heavy and massively wrought, frequently serving as knocker and handle in one, surmounted on a circular or shaped plate, pierced and ornamented in all sorts of quaint designs.

The examples of doorways illustrated from Bowmeadow Farm, Laverton, (Plate xliii), and Warren House, (Plate xl), at Stanton, though plain show the hinges and fastenings found on them.

The wrought iron work to the window casements was another opportunity for the exercise of the powers of the local smith. The variety of the shaped and perforated handle-plates seems endless and hardly any are found alike. Many contained the initials of the owner of the house, ingeniously worked into the design, as in the one illustrated, from a house near Broadway, where the letter S is the initial letter of Savage, who built the house.

All this iron work, both to doors and windows, was made by the local smith, doubtless from old traditional patterns, varied and altered to suit individual tastes.

The windows are always stone mullioned, filled with lead-latticed panes and wrought-iron casements (*see* Figs. 29 and 34).

They are nearly always treated in the same way, being 12 to 16 inches wide between the mullions, and 2 to 3 feet in height, while over the head, and returning at each side, they have the hollow label or drip moulding—a survival of earlier days.

Frequently this was carried round the building as a string course above the ground floor windows, as shown in the houses illustrated from St. Paul's Street, Stamford, (Plate xliv), the almshouses at Campden, (Plate x), and the cottages at Broadway (Plate xxvii).

Sometimes, as in the Northamptonshire examples, the label is put close above the window head, worked in the same stone, returning at each end as a cornice, (Plate lvii), while in Church Street, Stroud (Plate xlv) and in Cirencester (Plate xlvi) we see it carried almost the entire length of the building and terminated with a drip over each end window.

The number of lights in the windows in nearly every instance

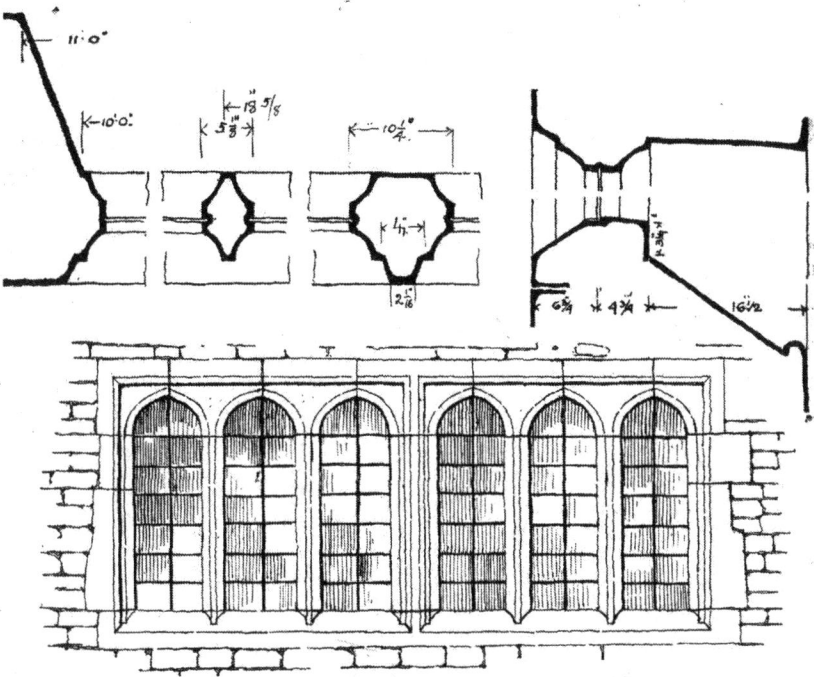

FIG. 28.   WINDOW AND DETAILS, S. EDWARD'S SCHOOL, STOW-ON-THE-WOLD.

diminishes in each succeeding storey. On the ground floor the windows have four, or sometimes six lights, with a heavier central mullion. The next storey will have three lights, and in the gable will be two. It was the invariable practice to lessen the number of lights as the windows ascend into the gables, as illustrated at

Withington, Broadway, Ramsden and Weston Subedge (Plates xlvii, xlviii, and xlix).

This simple treatment allowed great elasticity of arrangement, and so long as the windows were well proportioned, and were placed in good positions for lighting the rooms, they nearly always came in well with the external elevation.

The symmetrical disposition and squareness of the plans, and the way in which they were roofed in one span, enabled the windows to be easily arranged to come centrally under a gable in every case.

In many houses dating from the beginning of the seventeenth century we find the four-centred heads, as in the Warren House at Stanton, (Plate xxxix), where this treatment is also carried into the door, and at Stow-on-the-Wold, (Plate liii), in St. Edward's School all the windows are made so (*see* Fig. 28). This shaping of the window heads is an echo of the perpendicular work of the preceding century, and in some villages it lingered for a great many years, but as a rule it was confined to the doors only, and gradually the window with the square lintols became universal.

In the picturesque early sixteenth century house at Temple Guiting, (Plates liv and lv), for many years the summer residence of the Bishops of Oxford, the windows have these shaped heads, and a few years ago they were filled with glazing containing the arms of the bishop, or a mitre, a crozier, or other ecclesiastical symbol.

The windows in every case were placed on the outer face of the wall, so that inside the deep recess gives that delightful sense of comfort that is only to be found where thick walls are used.

Bay windows are not of very frequent occurrence in the smaller houses, but in the towns and village streets they are sometimes used with very happy effect, as in the illustration of the cottages at Yarwell, (Plate lvii), and at Duddington, in Northamptonshire (Plate lviii).

The house at Yarwell is of singularly pleasant proportion, and refined detail. The entrance was on the left side of the bay, which, with the gable above, is of dressed stone, contrasting with the general walling of thin layers of rubble. The whole front is tied together by a band of stone at the cill level.

When the frontage of the street was very narrow the entrance doorway was placed in the centre, with a bay window of flat projection on either side, terminating in a gable above. A very effective instance of this is seen in the *Swan Inn* at Lechlade, shown on Plate lx, in the other shop at Colley Weston, (Plate xxix), and in the houses in St. Paul's Street, at Stamford, (Plate xliv), which unfortunately loses much of its charm through having the intermediate mullions cut out. The houses in Chipping Campden, (Plate lxi), and Callowel near Stroud, (Plate lxii), have a doorway in the centre with windows and gables placed symmetrically on either side, giving very much the effect of the Lechlade example, without the bay treatment.

Sometimes the oriel window was used, corbeled out from the main wall, as shown in the illustration from Nassington in Northamptonshire, (Plate lxiii), and at Burford in Oxfordshire, (Fig. 83), but these can hardly be classed with the genuine Cotswold work, and are distinctly of earlier date.

Occasionally the bays are brought out square from the front of the house, as at Barford in Oxfordshire, (Plate lxiv), where the ground and first floor windows are alike in the number and treatment of the lights. An unusual way is the method of putting the bay in the centre of the gable, as at Lyddington in Northants, (Plate lxv), which is of three lights in width and finished with a gable at the top, but there is a sense of artificiality about the chimney stack rising from the main gable behind it that is not entirely pleasing.

No description of the windows would be complete without speaking of the dormers, the most characteristic feature of these Cotswold houses. Their origin, which is very simple, arose in the following manner. The buildings were roofed in a single span, generally commencing about 12 or 15 feet above the ground, or some 4 feet above the bedroom floor.

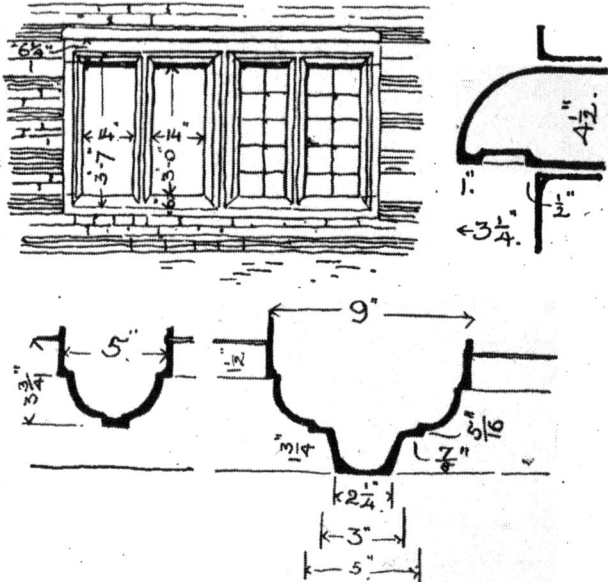

FIG. 29. WINDOW AT GRETTON, NORTHANTS.

This did not give height enough for windows to be placed under the eaves at the sides, and as the bedroom was always constructed partly in the roof, it was necessary to carry up the side walls and form a series of smaller gables, with windows in them.

These were treated in all respects similarly to the ordinary ones, finished either with a coping and finial, or else with a stone slate verge. In almost all the examples illustrated of these dormer windows are shown, but particular attention might be drawn to the charming effect of the farm-house at Willersey, Plate

IN THE COTSWOLD DISTRICT

v, and that at Little Rissington (Plate xiii).

A later type of dormer is occasionally seen, formed entirely in the roof, as illustrated in the Dean Row, Coln St. Aldwyn (Plate lxxv), and Medford House, (Plate lxxx), but they lack the charm of the earlier ones.

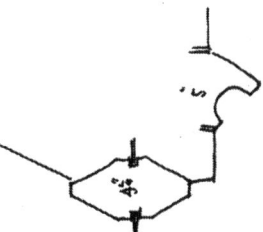

FIG. 30. TYPICAL HOLLOW "PERPENDICULAR" LABEL.

Another window also peculiar to this Cotswold district, though again of much later date, is that illustrated in the Baker's and Carpenter's Shops at Bourton-on-the-Hill, (Plates lxxvii and lxxviii), and in the cottage at Broadway (Plate lxxvi). Here we have a simple bay window with a stone base, above which is a framework of wood, and lead-lights, covered by a stone slated roof and generally accompanied by shutters, folding back against the wall on either side.

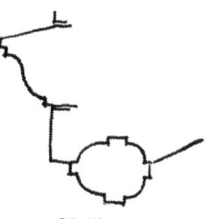

Mullions.

These windows are only found on the ground floor rooms, and are most picturesque additions to the houses they adorn.

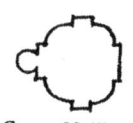

Centre Mullion.

There was during the 17th century a great similarity in the mouldings of domestic buildings, and this was so whether the houses were large or small.

The earliest form of moulding, and one that continued in use in a modified form longer than any others, was the hollow moulded mullion and jambs (*see* Fig. 28).

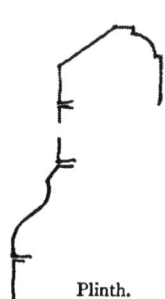

Plinth.

This usually accompanies the Tudor or Gothic-shaped head, as at Stow-on-the-Wold, (Plate liii), and was eventually superseded by the ovolo-shaped mullion, as in Fig. 29.

FIGS. 31, 32, 33. MOULDINGS FROM THE ALMSHOUSES, CAMPDEN.

34   OLD COTTAGES, FARM-HOUSES, &c.

The hollow " perpendicular " label was used indiscriminately with both these types, and lasted as long as any other features in the houses (*see* Fig. 30).

Occasionally the centre mullion—where six or four lights are used in one window, had the jamb moulding repeated as an additional fillet, (*see* Figs. 28 and 32), generally square but sometimes round as in the Almshouses at Campden, where the label moulding again varies (*see* Figs. 31–33).

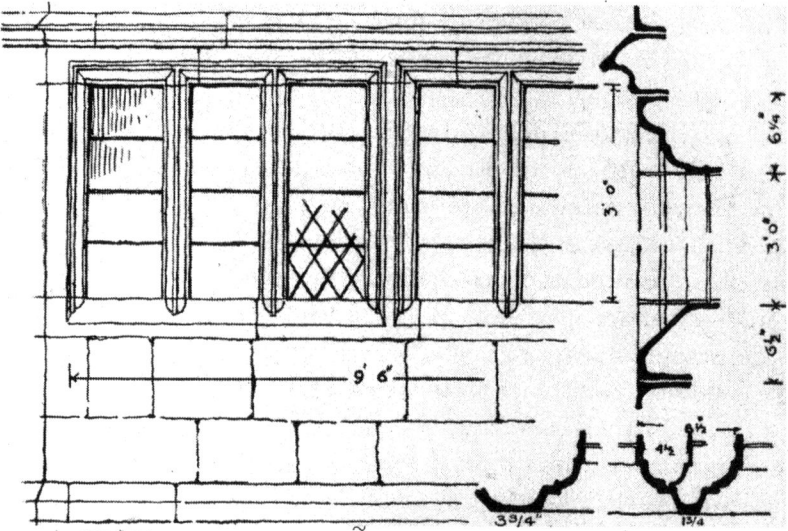

FIG. 34. WINDOW AND DETAILS AT WANSFORD, NORTHANTS.

The ordinary window detail was the plain chamfered mullion with the hollow moulding over, as shown in Fig. 30, and this was universal throughout the whole district for a great number of years, and is found even where the entire design of the house is altered, and almost every other detail changed, as at Medford House, Mickleton, (Plates lxxx to lxxxiii), where the windows are practically the only features retaining the old traditional forms.

The sizes of the stonework to the windows is invariably the

IN THE COTSWOLD DISTRICT

same, the mullions some 5 inches to 5¾ inches wide, with the larger central one anything between 7 inches and 9 inches, the heads about 7 inches to 8 inches in depth, the cills shallower, and the hollow label over, some 4 inches deep, returning on either side the depth of the head. Every village mason knew and kept to these proportions, and consequently repeated them time after time.

With the gradual change in style towards the end of the seventeenth century and the introduction of classic detail, the lights became wider and higher, and as the rooms too became loftier, transomes and upper lights were inserted, as will be seen in the example on Plate ix.

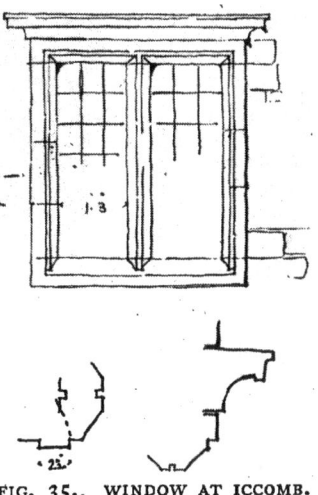

FIG. 35. WINDOW AT ICCOMB.

In Burford there is a very charming house, dated 1672, facing the main street, which contains some extremely pleasing detail of this transitional period, where the mullion style still prevailed, but evidencing the endeavour to graft the newer fashion on the older forms.

At Colley Weston in Northants is another variety, where the mullions are still ovolo moulded, but with a hollow treated as an architrave all round, dying out on to a projecting splayed cill, and covered by a cornice over the head.

The example from Iccomb in Gloucestershire, (Fig. 35), is plainer; here the chamfered mullion and jambs are used, but all round a raised fillet forms an architrave from which a hollow moulded cornice springs.

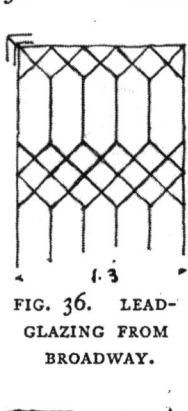

FIG. 36. LEAD-GLAZING FROM BROADWAY.

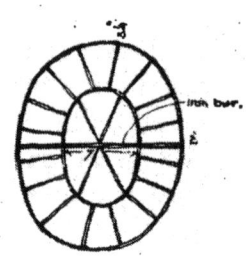

FIG. 38. AN OVAL WINDOW FROM MICKLETON.

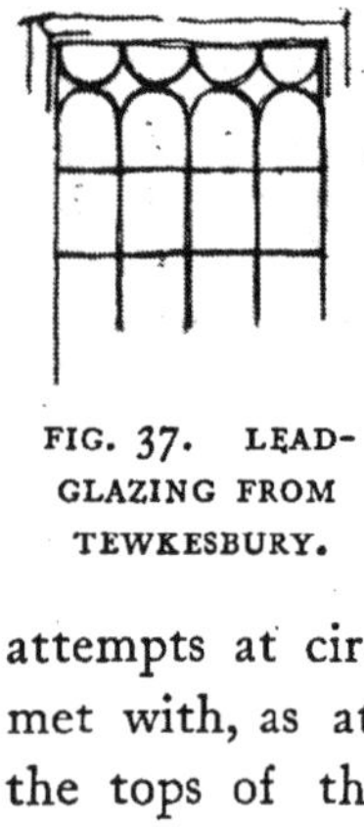

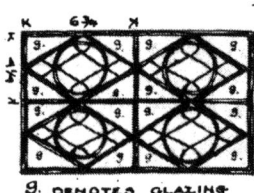

FIG. 37. LEAD-GLAZING FROM TEWKESBURY.

FIG. 39. LEADED VENTILATOR FROM A HOUSE NEAR CAMPDEN.

The lead latticed glazing of these houses forms quite an integral part of their construction, and a stone-mullioned window without its accompanying small panes of glass is but a sorry sight.

In the earlier houses we find the diamond panes, or patterns based upon a variation of the diamond and square, sometimes very small and intricate, as in Fig. 36 from Broadway, but always such as the village glazier could cut and put together. Any attempts at circular or interlacing leading are only occasionally met with, as at Winchcombe and Tewkesbury, (Fig. 37), where the tops of the lights are rounded, giving a little variation to the monotony of the square panes.

Towards the middle of the seventeenth century the rectangular oblong panes became very popular, and continued so down to the close of the eighteenth with but little change; indeed it is doubtful if any form of latticed lights were so suitable with either stone or wooden mullioned windows.

The oval windows in the gables were occasionally filled with patterned leading as at Mickleton, (Fig. 38), and sometimes in dairies and such places the lead was left unglazed for ventilation—a

IN THE COTSWOLD DISTRICT 37

quaint example being given from a house near Campden (Fig. 39).

Here, as in everything else in the district, the ingenuity and spontaneous originality of the craftsman is very marked. This was doubtless a pattern worked out by himself, and though it does not pretend to anything in the way of design, yet the forms selected are suitable and it serves its purpose admirably, besides giving a pleasant touch of character to the window it fills.

The colour of the old glass again is noticeable, varying from pale amber to bottle green; somewhat unsuitable for seeing through, as it distorts the vista outside in a painful manner, but yet seeming to adapt itself to the old stone windows in a way that quite clear glass perhaps would not do.

The leading of the small panes of glass always enabled the texture of the masonry walls to be carried, as it were, through the windows without a break, getting a continuity of surface that is very pleasing, and which these old builders thoroughly appreciated.

The mistake so many people make to-day is in glazing the windows, with single sheets of glass, producing a cold effect inside and breaking up the exterior with cavernous spots of black, and emphasizing the mullions in a manner that was never intended.

It would of course be wearisome and profitless to go through the category of trifling variations of the detail of doors and windows, as they differed but little from those in general use all over the country, and where they did the changes were evidently attributable to the whim and ingenuity of the mason, who wanted to be in the fashion and adopt the newer styles, and who having probably once seen them in other parts of the country, interpreted them in his own work as best he could.

In dealing with the subject of windows, the panel decorations placed over them in the gables must not be overlooked.

These, like most other features in the houses, were distinctly

38 OLD COTTAGES, FARM-HOUSES, &c.

local in their treatment, consisting in many instances of merely a small single light, either filled with glass or made solid.

In Northamptonshire, as a glance at the illustrations will show, they were nearly always either square or diamond-shaped panels containing a date and initials, as at the *White Lion* at Oundle (Plate xciii), St. Paul's Street, Stamford, shown in Figs. 40 and 41, or else projecting with a moulded cornice above, as at Colley Weston, (Plate xxix), and occasionally taking the form of a shield as at Nassington (Plate lxvii).

In the neighbourhood of Broadway, the oval or circular form was universal, the opening bordered with a series of small rustications. This treatment was evidently popular and lasted for many years, as the examples at Paxford, (Plate lxx), Willersey, (Plate lxxxiv), and Stanton, (Plate iv), show, and it appears again on either side of the central window in the front of Medford House at Mickleton, (Plate lxxx), a very charming composition, many years later in date than the other examples.

FIG. 40. A GABLE IN S. PAUL'S STREET, STAMFORD.

IN THE COTSWOLD DISTRICT

These openings were doubtless originally glazed, as in the case of the small opening at Top Farm, Broadway, (*see* Fig. 42), and in the house just referred to, but often they are found plastered up on the outside. Sometimes, as at Weston Subedge, the panel took the form of a plain sinking with a curved head, (Plate xxxviii), and the form of two lancet lights cut out of a single stone, as at Stanton, (*see* Fig. 43), is not uncommon.

FIG. 41. PANEL FROM THE GABLE AT STAMFORD HILL.

At first sight this looks like some early thirteenth century work inserted in the more modern building, but a closer inspection reveals the handiwork of the seventeenth century village craftsman.

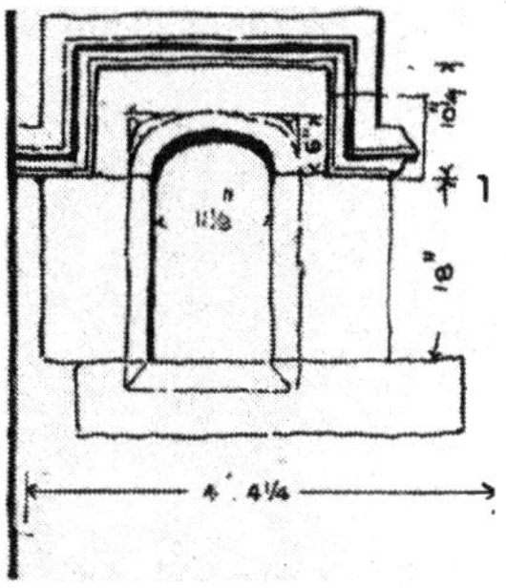

In the Stroud district a favourite form was the round cut out of one piece of square stone, as at the *Plough* at Callowel (Plate lxii), and in many of the larger houses designs of more pretentious character are often seen.

FIG. 42. GABLE OPENING, TOP FARM, BROADWAY.

Square stones, built in flush with the walling, and bearing a date and initials, either sunk or raised, were very popular, and were generally placed over the doorway and sometimes worked in the actual lintol itself.

These tablets, generally of the seventeenth and eighteenth centuries, in some form or other, either enriched or plain, are found more or less all through these districts following the belt of limestone,

FIG. 43. AT STANTON.

that traverses England diagonally from the Dorsetshire to the Yorkshire coasts (*see* Figs. 44 to 49).

Where brick or wood are the ordinary building materials, it is seldom that such tablets are seen, but stone offered a ready material

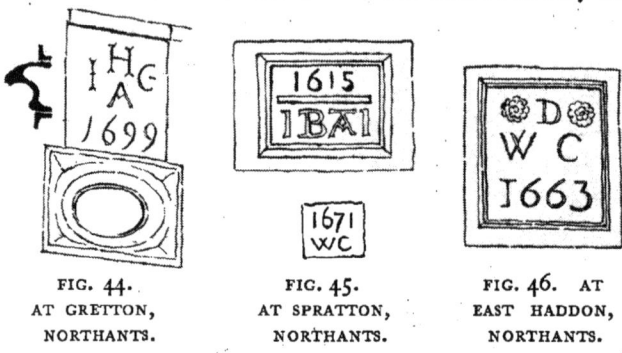

FIG. 44.
AT GRETTON,
NORTHANTS.

FIG. 45.
AT SPRATTON,
NORTHANTS.

FIG. 46. AT
EAST HADDON,
NORTHANTS.

at hand for the easy exercise of local fancy, and much quaint ingenuity was displayed in the fashioning of them.

They are doubtless a lingering survival of the old custom of

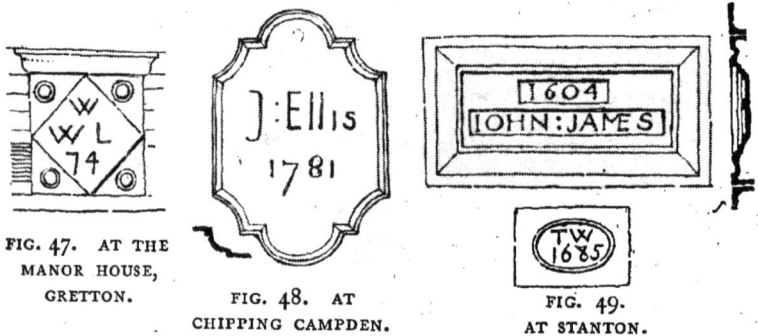

FIG. 47. AT THE
MANOR HOUSE,
GRETTON.

FIG. 48. AT
CHIPPING CAMPDEN.

FIG. 49.
AT STANTON.

placing the owner's coat of arms over the entrance door, and are interesting if only for that reason.

The simplest form is just a slab of stone, with the initials and date upon it, within a panel, the disposition of the initials generally following one fashion—that of the surname at the top—the Christian names of the man and his wife beneath, and the date at the bottom.

These stones are very frequently seen upon the houses in Gloucestershire and Northants, sometimes two and even more being on the same house, showing the changes of occupation they have undergone at different periods (*see* Fig. 49).

It seems a pity that so simple a means of adding some small amount of interest and individuality to the entrance of a house should be but seldom seen now-a-days, but like most other local customs this is rapidly dying out.

In the smaller houses, as the rooms were usually about 7 or 8 feet high, the windows were always one light in height, and it was only towards the end of the century, and in the larger buildings, that a transome and upper light became common.

It is the lowness of the storeys, and the length of the windows, that give the charming sense of good proportion common to nearly all these small houses and cottages, for though the old builders may have had but rudimentary ideas upon the soundness of building, they have never been excelled as regards the beautiful and simple proportions of their houses.

Although they were all built on traditional lines and well-recognized principles, yet we may traverse the district from end to end and not find two houses exactly alike.

The style was elastic, and the arrangement of the roofs enabled the builders to dispose of the windows and gables as they pleased. It is this infinite diversity of form and variety of treatment that make these stone-built houses stand out so pre-eminently as a phase of domestic architecture, quite apart from anything else in the country.

If we turn to the plan of the house at Aston Subedge, (*see* Fig. 50), we find it consists of one simple parallelogram. The main doorway, (*see* Fig. 51), is in the centre, with a room immediately right and left of it, and through the latter a smaller one, the back kitchen or brew-house.

The original staircase was by the chimney, which contains two wide fireplaces.

As the ground falls from right to left a series of steps lead out of the porch into the smaller living room, which has an additional outer doorway.

This house is now used as the village school, and its interior

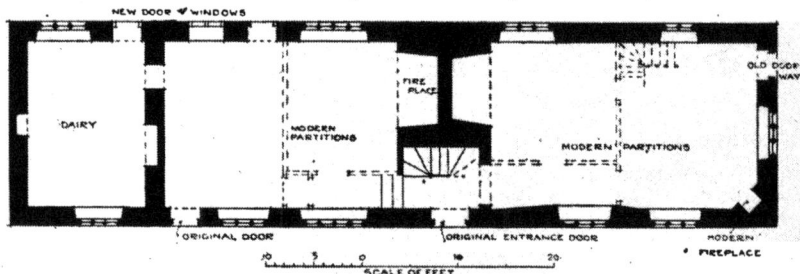

FIG. 50. PLAN OF HOUSE AT ASTON SUBEDGE (NOW THE VILLAGE SCHOOL).

has been considerably altered by partitions, but the simplicity of the original plan is reflected in the elevation, which shows a roof unbroken from end to end, with the exception of two small gables over the entrance doorway, and the window beside it.

The farmhouse at Willersey, (Plate v), has a somewhat similar plan with a series of windows carried up as dormers into the roof above, all thoroughly well balanced and giving on the exterior a clue to the arrangement of the rooms within. The heights and widths of the windows, and the disposal of the gables, leave nothing to be desired. The whole composition, free from any

IN THE COTSWOLD DISTRICT

striving after effect, is an example of simple direct building and a lesson in the sensible use of material.

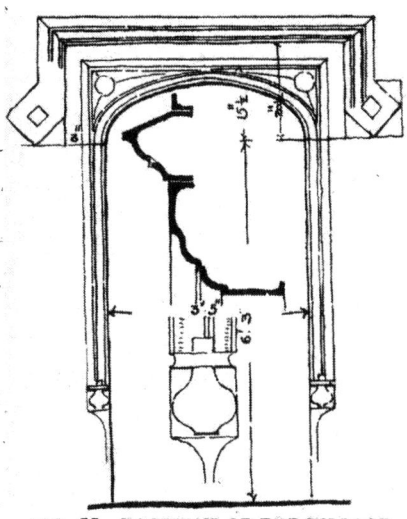

FIG. 51. DOORWAY OF THE VILLAGE SCHOOL, ASTON SUBEDGE.

The chimneys are amongst the most characteristic features of these Cotswold houses, and are invariably carried up, massive and solid, and suggest wide ingle nooks and cosy firesides, as in the instance shown from Medford House at Mickleton, (Plate lxxxiii), where the stack is taken up the full width and is finished with a roof having the chimney in the centre of the gable.

The stacks at Snowshill, (Plate xxvi), the Warren House at Stanton, (Plate xxxix), the cottages at Ebrington, (Plate lxxxv), at Humphries Farm, near Stroud, (Plate lxxxvi), and Woodchester (Plate lxxxvii), are typical of the external treatment of the fireplaces.

They were always placed centrally over the ridge or on the apex of the gables at either end, and when the stacks were at the sides of the building, then on smaller roofs connecting them with the main one, as in the house at Weston Subedge (Plate xxxviii).

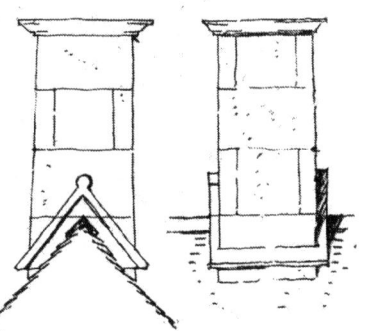

FIG. 52. STACKS AT BROADWAY.

The chimney-stack immediately above the roof, and up to the base moulding, was invariably square, while on the other side, and coinciding with the gable coping, is a projecting weather course, under which the slates were tucked, and which also returned along the bottom edge (*see* Fig. 52). This treatment, which is invariable with the stone roofs, can be seen in numerous houses, and is shown at Weston Subedge, (Plate xxxviii), at Temple Guiting, (Plates liv and lv), and Broadway (Plate xxxi).

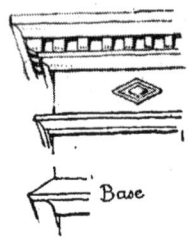

FIG. 53. CAP OF A BROADWAY CHIMNEY.

When the roof is cleared, the flues are often built separately, either square or diagonally, in clusters of three or four, always made of slabs of sawn and dressed stone, about three or four inches thick, and eight or ten inches in depth, standing on edge and breaking joint over each other, tied together at the top by a moulded stone cap of simple section, as at Withington, (Plate xlvii), and Broadway (Plate xxxi).

Sometimes this cap was treated as a cornice with architrave and frieze, enriched with sunk patterns, raised diamonds, or other devices that took the mason's fancy, as in the house at Broadway, (*see* Fig. 53), and at Campden (Plate xxxii). Fig. 56 gives some characteristic sections of these cornice-

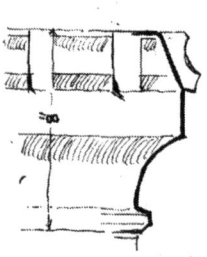

FIG. 54. AT STANTON.

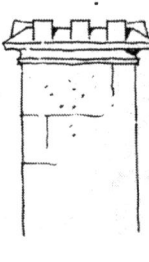

FIG. 55. AT BURFORD.

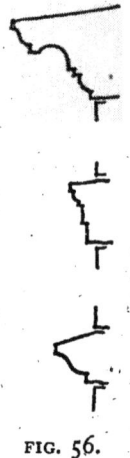

FIG. 56. TYPICAL PROFILES OF CHIMNEY CORNICES.

IN THE COTSWOLD DISTRICT

cappings. Occasionally the earlier Gothic treatment is seen, where we find the battlemented top as at Stanton and Burford, (Figs. 54 and 55), but these are somewhat isolated instances and only emphasize, by their rarity, the frequency with which the others were used.

Many of the earlier chimneys still remain in this part of the country, some incorporated in work of a later date. These generally consist of octagonal or circular shafts pierced with lancet openings, crowned at the top with a pyramidal roof, as in those illustrated from Kingham, Bredon, and Bibury (Figs. 57, 58, and 59).

FIG. 57. CHIMNEY FROM KINGHAM.

In the arrangements of the roofs too the old Cotswold builders greatly excelled, and here we find the most characteristic features of their buildings.

If we analyse them in order to discover what constitutes their charm, we find that they resolve themselves into very simple forms, but the masterly way in which, in almost every instance, the grouping and disposal of the gables, dormers, and chimney-stacks was managed is worthy of admiration.

FIG. 58. CHIMNEY ON A BARN AT BREDON, WORC.

FIG. 59. CHIMNEY FROM BIBURY.

The roofs were nearly always treated in the same way, having a fairly steep pitch, of about 55 degrees, and being hung with stone slates, graduated in thickness from the eaves to the ridge, where the thinnest and smallest are placed, and crowned on the top with a stone cresting of some simple section.

Here we see the effect of material upon design and construction, and how these old country builders realized that one was dependent on the other.

The nature of the stone of which the slates, or "slats," as they are locally called, were made, limits them to certain sizes, so that the stone roofs of somewhat low pitch, with the large and heavy slates found in Sussex and the North of England, are quite unknown here.

As soon as the angle of the roof was flattened the slates had to be larger, for the small slates would not keep the wet out, and so after finding the exact pitch at which they had least strain on the pins and were most weather proof, the old slates never varied it.

The names of the slates are exceedingly quaint, and doubtless have their origin in very remote times, but the slaters are chary of using them before strangers, and it is only amongst themselves that one hears them spoken. The bottom or under slates at the eaves—the one bedded on the top of the walls—is called a "cussome." This has a slight tilt downwards, to throw the water off, and projects some seven or eight inches. Above this the eaves commence with long and short "eighteens" down to long and short "elevens"; then we have long and short "wivetts," "becks," "bachelors," "movedays," "cuttings," and long and short "cocks" at the apex under the cresting.

They are hung dry with oak or deal pegs, which are driven tight into holes in the slates, whilst they are being sorted to sizes, or else nailed in the ordinary manner. When plastered or torched with hair mortar, level with the underside of the laths, they will last for years, as so many existing buildings testify.

The "valleys" are formed of the same slates, in a wide sweep with no hard line of demarcation where the roofs intersect, laid in regular formation and ranging with the ordinary slating.

Each valley slate has its distinctive name, the centre one being the "bottomer," with two "lie-byes" on either side, and above and below in the next courses two "skews" to break joint. Numerous examples of this work in the roofs, are shown in the plates, as for instance Nos. 27 and 94.

There are of course only certain districts where the stone from which these slates are made is found. It has to easily laminate in thin beds, to be hard and weather resisting, and without sand-holes or flaws.

In Northamptonshire there is a bed of stone, at Colley Weston and Easton, which laminates very freely, and has formed from a very early period the prevalent roofing material of the locality. These Northamptonshire slates, as a rule, are of a larger size than the Oxford and Gloucestershire ones, obtained at the celebrated Stonesfield and Guiting and Eyford Quarries, but all are equally durable and weather resisting.

The method of getting the slates is interesting, as it differs from the general custom of splitting by hand.

In October a piece of ground at the quarry is measured off and the upper eight or ten feet of loose "brash" is cleared away, this process being called "ridding." The "pendal," as the stone for the slates is called, is then uncovered and wheeled to the top of the ground, laid down flat, and roughly fitted together as nearly as it will allow, in thicknesses varying from two to twelve or fourteen inches, just as it comes from the quarry.

It has then to lie and wait for the winter frosts, which swell the beds of natural moisture in the "pendal," and when a thaw sets in, a few blows of the hammer soon separate the layers, which are then cut to the sizes required and sorted ready for use. But should the winters be mild, the stone has to wait until the following year.

The ridge cresting or "crease," as it is locally called, was sawn out of a block of stone in a very simple and economical way. A piece of stone nine inches or ten inches wide and about two or three feet long is stood on edge, and a series of saw cuts in the form of a V made in it from end to end, the pieces are then lifted out, the top sharp arris and bottom edges squared off, and the ridge is ready for use. By this means a comparatively small piece of stone will make sufficient cresting to cover a very large quantity of roofing. (Figs. 60 and 61 show this method.)

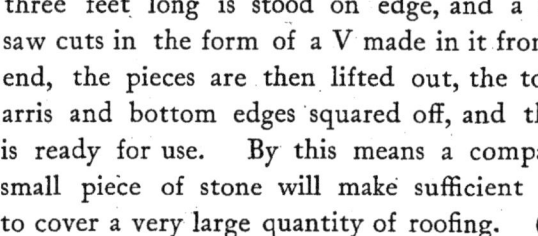

FIGS. 60, 61. METHOD OF FORMING RIDGE CRESTING.

Owing possibly to the cost or difficulty of procuring lead in these country towns and villages, the builders did without it, and the houses, as mentioned before, however large or small, were always planned so that they could be roofed in one single span.

Hips, or any cutting or mitreing of the slates was absolutely unknown in a genuine stone-roofed house, and there are invariably gables with the slates carried out over them to form a verge, or butting, up to and tucked under the stone coping. Even at the junction of a lower roof with a higher one, where the ridge dies in, no lead was used, but a length of cresting was turned upside down to throw the water off, as shown in the inn at Willersey, (Plate lxxxiv), or the cottage at Bourton-on-the-Hill (Plate lxxviii).

IN THE COTSWOLD DISTRICT

The old craftsmen could do almost anything with these stone slates. The clever way in which the outside ovens are roofed, with the slates worked up on the curve as at Snowshill, (Plate xxvi), or over the circular outer staircases with pointed roofs, and again in the beautiful dovecots, of which so many still remain scattered about the country side is truly remarkable. A good example of these is still standing at Bibury; it is circular, with a later cupola addition on the top (*see* Fig. 62). Another at Southrop shows the traditional gabled treatment with four equal sides.

In this latter instance we see how successfully the roofs were treated, for a simple square on plan, roofed as this is, produces a building full of charm, and gives effects of light and shade that perhaps no other form of roof could.

FIG. 62. DOVECOTE AT BIBURY.

It is interesting to note here a wall at Stow-on-the-Wold in which the pigeon holes have been built at regular intervals, as shown in Fig. 63.

Then again the way in which difficulties were got over is always instructive.

In many buildings we find the stone bays, with canted sides carried up to the eaves without any awkward problems to solve, but as soon as the roof was reached it meant either a lead flat and parapet, or else some way of getting back into a flat gable, and many and ingenious were the means adopted to attain this.

Sometimes it was clumsily managed, but at Lechlade is seen the simplest possible way, (Plate lx), while in other cases, as in the Northamptonshire examples, the junctions between the canted sides of the bay and the gable over, were made a specially delightful feature, as shown in Fig. 40. But however it was treated the full gable overhanging the sides is never quite satisfactory, always having a certain sense of weakness and makeshift, never seen in the gable over the square bay.

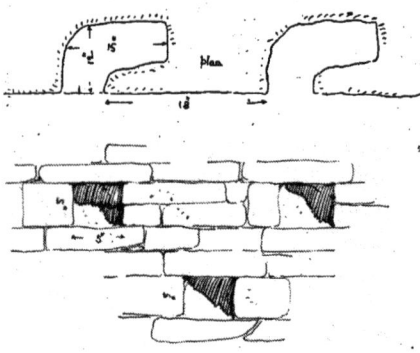

FIG. 63. PIGEON HOLES IN THE WALL, STOW-ON-THE-WOLD.

For stone houses there is no more beautiful or suitable material than these slates as a roof covering, which harmonize so admirably, and seem almost to grow from the walls supporting them. When old and covered with lichens their colour is indescribably exquisite, and seen in their proper setting amidst trees and fields the general tone of silver grey harmonizes admirably with the surrounding landscape. Even when new they are pleasing, as the slates are of all shades of greys, browns, and yellows.

Unfortunately, owing to the advent of railways and cheap means of locomotion, the purple blue Welsh slates, and even galvanised iron, are now becoming common. Both materials are doubtless good in themselves, but they are out of all harmony with the buildings, and do not in any way blend with them.

Such "foreign" materials possibly have the advantage of being cheaper and easier to carry, the stone slates requiring slightly heavier timbering, more care and trouble in fixing, and occasional repairing. But these are poor reasons to set against the fact that houses and barns two hundred and more years old still stand covered with their original roofs.

The slates, if properly seasoned at first, are almost imperishable, for no frost or wet will touch them; they can be taken off and re-hung again and again, and as a consequence old ones command a ready sale and are eagerly sought for.

It seems unreasonable to go miles afield to obtain an inferior, if cheaper, material, when the better one lies literally at one's feet, but this now happens, and as a result it becomes more and more difficult to get slaters who understand the work, as the craft, like that of the thatcher, seems to be dying out for lack of employment.

Many of the modern stone slates are not so good as the old, not by reason of any failing in the quality of the stone, but simply from the demand for mechanical precision which seems to pervade all trades to-day.

They are now made as smooth and thin as possible, and with all the edges dressed square and true, and when hung look hard and cold and but little different, except in colour, from a blue slate roof; possessing none of the softness and texture of the old roofs. Nor are they so durable, the old slates being rough and uneven, never laid close, and the wet and moisture soon dried out of them; but the new ones, closely fitted and bedded tight down, one on the other, the circulation of air between them is prevented and the wet retained much longer, giving a better chance to frost.

In a great degree this is due to the irregularity of the old

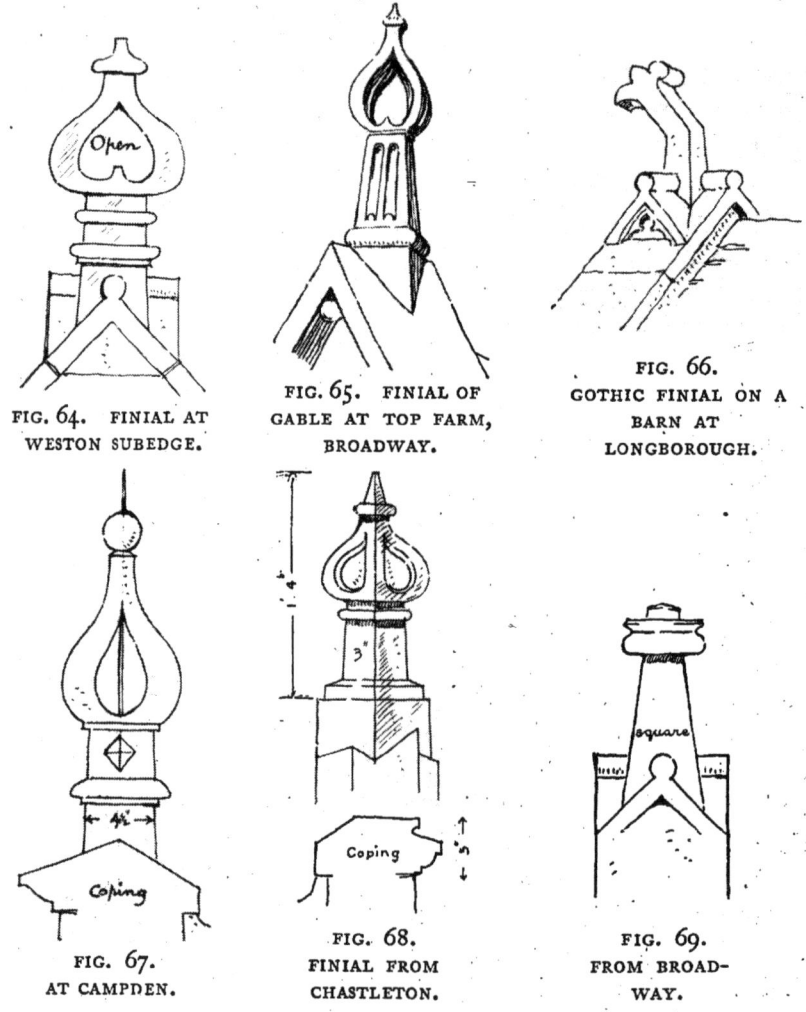

FIG. 64. FINIAL AT WESTON SUBEDGE.

FIG. 65. FINIAL OF GABLE AT TOP FARM, BROADWAY.

FIG. 66. GOTHIC FINIAL ON A BARN AT LONGBOROUGH.

FIG. 67. AT CAMPDEN.

FIG. 68. FINIAL FROM CHASTLETON.

FIG. 69. FROM BROADWAY.

IN THE COTSWOLD DISTRICT

slates, which gives such a texture to the surface of the roofs and which one so sadly misses in many new ones. The old slates were always thick and rough, with irregularities of surface and uneven edges, and the old oak riven laths, on which the slates were hung, not being always straight, the bottom edges varied and did not carry a hard straight line, thus giving a charmingly diversified effect.

In connection with the roofs the variety of the gable termi-

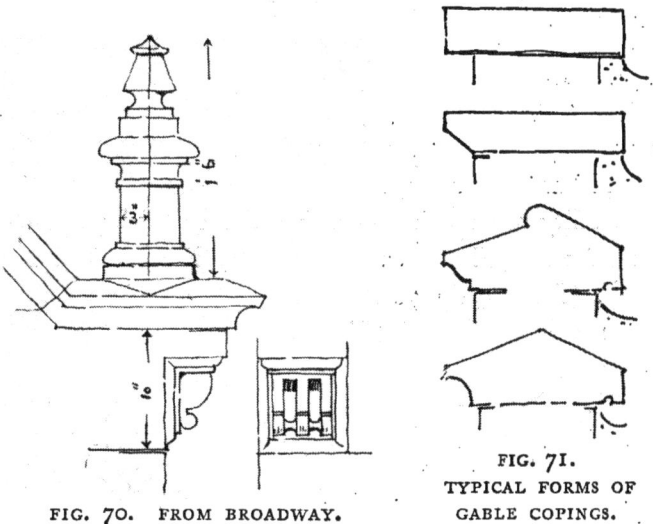

FIG. 70. FROM BROADWAY.

FIG. 71.
TYPICAL FORMS OF GABLE COPINGS.

nations is very worthy of notice, for perhaps in no district of England is such diversity of form and detail found.

They are generally placed on the apex of the gables, but sometimes on the springers as well, and many are pierced and cut in a delightful manner (*see*, inter alia, Figs. 64, 65 and 70). They are found all through the stone districts, but in the neighbourhood of Campden, the villages round, and in parts of Northants, there are some extremely pleasing examples.

These finials express as much as anything else the individuality of the men who made them. In every village and town, as before mentioned, the style of building and proportions were almost traditional, and there was little or no departure from it, but these

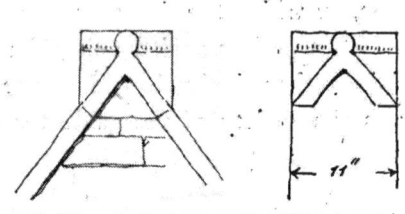

FIG. 72. GABLE TERMINATION FROM SNOWSHILL.

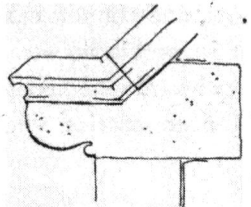

FIG. 73. GABLE TERMINATION FROM WINCHCOMBE.

finials were little instances of personal detail that the country mason let himself go upon, and some are much stronger and more full of vitality than others—notice the excellent open ones at Weston Subedge, (Fig. 64), and Willersey, (Fig. 68), and Top Farm Broadway, (Figs. 65, 69, 70), and the early Gothic example on the tithe barn at Longborough (Fig. 66).

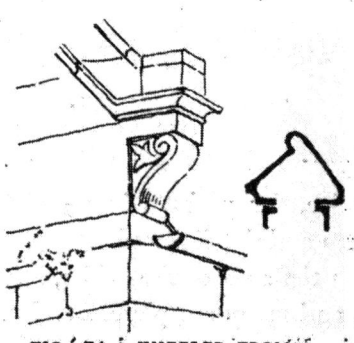

FIG. 74. KNEELER FROM DEDDINGTON, OXON.

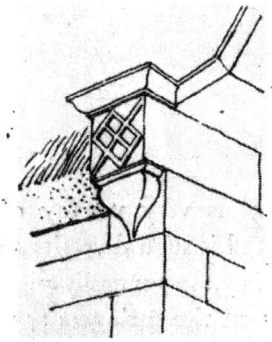

FIG. 75. KNEELER FROM GRETTON, NORTHANTS.

The gable copings also are of simple outline; those to the more unpretentious cottages being no more than a flat stone projecting slightly, back and front, with the slates tucked closely under behind—others again have a more Gothic outline. We find many and various ways of treating the springing apex generally quite plain—sometimes as at Snowshill, (Fig. 72), and sometimes as at Deddington, (Fig. 74), and Gretton, (Fig. 75), and Broadway (Fig. 76).

The examples shown in many of the Northamptonshire houses are quite unique, and are rather different from the Cotswold ones.

A very frequent and favourite treatment is to reverse the apex with a small cusped opening under, and kept quite plain, (*see* Fig. 75), an echo of earlier perpendicular tradition. Sometimes this was on the actual ridge cresting itself, when no stone coping was used, as at Callowel Farm (Plate xciv).

In many of the houses all through the Cotswolds there are small features of this kind, emphasizing the thoughtful way in which the builders settled the problems they had to deal with.

Of timber-built houses, we do not find in the hill country any large amount, but directly we get off the stone and into the valleys, where oak was grown, we find half timber and plaster houses, and these combined with the stonework make most picturesque buildings.

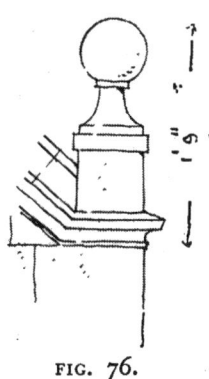

FIG. 76.
AT BROADWELL.

Under the slopes of the Bredon Hills there are whole villages in which this treatment is adopted, and it is found in the Stroud valley, as at Leonard Stanley, (Plate c), and again in the Warwickshire vale. All these places are bordering on the stone districts, and in all a mixture of the two materials is met with.

Plaster or rough cast houses are somewhat plentiful, though it is questionable whether this rough cast—which is generally of eighteenth century date—was not, on the stone houses at any rate, used as a protection against the driving rain, which in this part of the country penetrates even these thick stone walls.

In the houses at Burford, (Plates xcvi and xcvii), it is doubtless put on over the timber framing below, and at Woodchester, (Plate lxxxvii), a stone-built house is so treated.

At Winchcombe, Stow-on-the-Wold, Cirencester, etc., there are numerous instances of this kind of work, in which imitation quoins are stamped at the angles and around the windows.

A very fine house at Stow-on-the-Wold, now unfortunately pulled down, had the front covered with geometrical patterns in plaster, with raised mouldings, diapers and patterns of a type not found in other districts and possessing a distinct individuality (*see* Fig. 77).

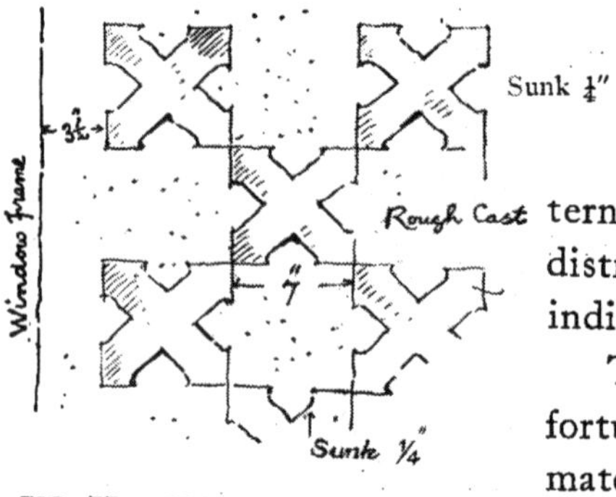

The bulk of this work is unfortunately only executed in a material that will not withstand the weather, and sad havoc is being wrought with much of what still remains.

FIG. 77. PLASTER PATTERNS FORMERLY ON A HOUSE AT STOW-ON-THE-WOLD.

In the smaller houses and cottages, though the general fabric was precisely similar to the manor houses, and the detail of doors and windows, chimneys and roofs was the same, the treatment of the interior was much simplified, and but little ornament or decoration is met with.

Instead of richly-panelled walls and delicately-fashioned plaster ceilings, we find plastered walls and roughly-hewn joists of oak or elm, with only occasionally a moulded beam.

IN THE COTSWOLD DISTRICT

Occasionally there are plaster ceilings, panelled rooms, and decorated fireplaces, but though these have suffered from rough usage and neglect, yet the workmanship of everything, however plain or simple, inside these houses was always the same, thoroughly honest and good.

It seemed to be a maxim that every house, irrespective of its

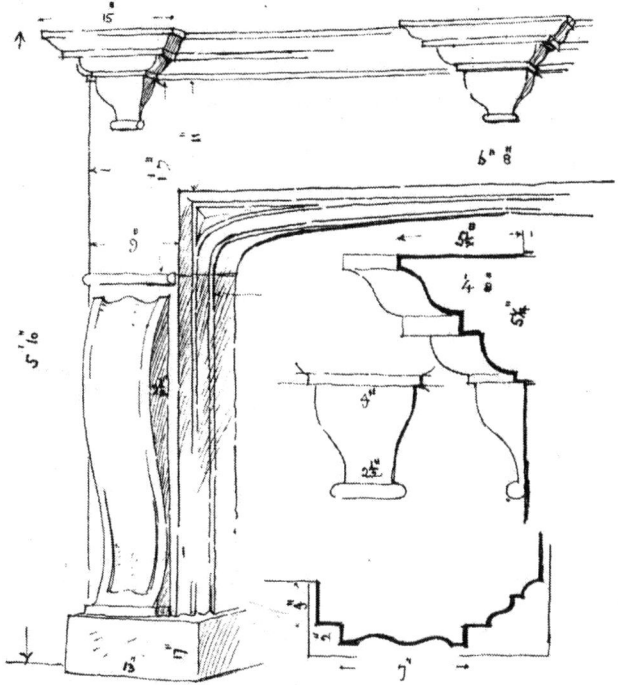

FIG. 78. STONE CHIMNEYPIECE, MANOR HOUSE, TURKDEAN, DATED 1588.

size, should be of the best workmanship and contain some work of interest and charm.

It must be remembered, however, that most of the larger houses were not in the first instance built as farmhouses and cottages, but having fallen on evil days, they have arrived at their present condition and occupation.

In the great houses, after the shell was built, it often happened that strange workmen were imported to execute the internal finishings, but in the simple buildings, where the work was plain it was all done by local workmen and with native home-grown material, and always has a dignity and simple charm that is very pleasing.

As we noticed before, it was on the fireplace and its surroundings that any little display of architectural design was generally lavished, and in some of the houses quite decorative treatments were adopted. The fireplace and chimneypiece at Turkdean, (*see* Fig. 78), is an instance of a somewhat unusual character, whilst that at Darlingscott, shown in Fig. 79, is of the commoner type.

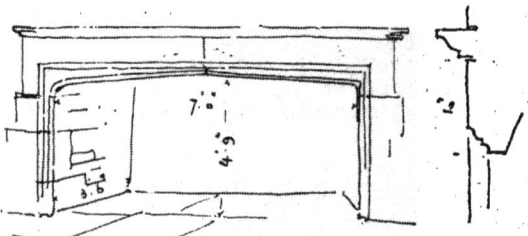

FIG. 79. FIREPLACE AT DARLINGSCOTT.

Wood was the universal fuel, so that fires were always on the hearth, and hence we find hardly any wrought iron work, with the exception of the fireplace where the cooking was done.

There is a good deal of characteristic building of late date, and many of the houses and cottages have been added to in Queen Anne's reign.

One typical example of a building of this date is Medford House, near Campden, (Plates lxxx to lxxxiii), of which the plan is given in Fig. 80.

Here a more symmetrical arrangement has been adopted, the

entrance being placed in the centre, with slightly projecting wings on either side.

The windows are the usual stone mullioned ones, traditional in detail, but the pedimented doorway, dentilled cornice and hipped roofs all show the classical influence of the times.

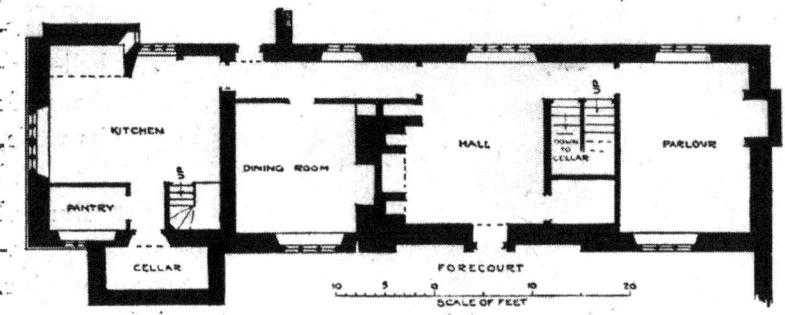

FIG. 80. PLAN OF MEDFORD HOUSE, MICKLETON.

The squareness of the entrance court, flanked by piers with well-designed urns, (*see* Fig. 81), is quite a departure from the haphazard though picturesque approaches to the ordinary houses.

Painswick and the Stroud valley contain many remarkably fine specimens of Queen Anne and Early Georgian work,—indeed it is freely scattered throughout all the towns and villages, but such work hardly falls within the scope of these notes, and merits a study by itself.

The ancient town of Burford is situated on the borders of Oxfordshire, and like many villages in the Cotswolds, lies in one of the narrow valleys that intersect the hills in all directions.

The surrounding country is typical of the whole district, with its wide stretches of bare uplands, dotted with groups of beech and elm trees and grey homesteads. The old town is similar to many others, with its broad and open High Street, scrupulously clean, and bordered by quaint houses of all ages and styles.

Fifty years ago it was a thriving and prosperous place, but the advent of railways has long since left it high and dry and out of the world of to-day. It was once renowned for the manufacture of paper, malt, sail cloth, saddlery and bell-casting. But though it has lost all its trade, and activity and bustle, yet Burford of to-day is a peaceful spot to visit. Like all these towns, it once played its part in history, and during the Civil Wars King Charles I was several times there. Queen Elizabeth hunted in Wychwood forest, and William III spent his birthday there in 1695 on his way to Oxford.

FIG. 81. ENTRANCE PIER AT MEDFORD HOUSE, MICKLETON.

Burford is well known for its Manor House, built about the year 1600 by Sir Lawrence Tanfield, whose monument is now in the church. The history of the house is indeed the history of Burford, but can hardly be considered as belonging to the class of smaller houses.

IN THE COTSWOLD DISTRICT 61

The church is probably unique, and its size and magnificence give some idea of what must have been the importance of the place in the Middle Ages. The town contains numerous interesting buildings; one of which is the old Tolsey House (Plate xcvii). It dates from the fifteenth century, and stands in the centre of the town. It originally stood on stone columns and was open below, but the spaces have been filled in some long time back. The tolls due to the Lord of the Manor, and those incurred by strangers at the fairs, used to be paid in this building, and there still remain in a room upstairs the old chairs, muniment boxes and chest of drawers with the town arms engraved upon them.

The house immediately opposite, of fifteenth century date, is well worth attention, (Plate xcvi), with its three gables, beautiful traceried barge boards, projecting oriel windows, and great pent roof over the shop-fronts below. Inside there is a fine chimney-piece, and, in the courtyard behind, the original wooden windows with arched heads, and a fine timber and plaster front with coved plaster cornice under the eaves.

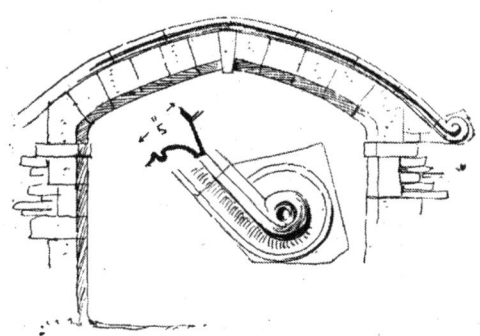

FIG. 82. ARCHWAY ENTRANCE AT BURFORD.

It was at one time all one house, and the perpendicular windows in the back gable facing the east may have been connected with an oratory chapel on the first floor.

Burford in the time of the Middle Ages must have been full of fascinating buildings, for on all sides are moulded and carved doorways, some of stone and several bearing dates, initials and merchants' marks of the original builders. As a rule the older houses, dating from the time of Henry VIII and Elizabeth, had an arched entrance facing the street, opening into a passage with the rooms leading off it on either side (*see* Fig. 82). This passage further led into a courtyard at the back, and in many of the later buildings the old circular outer staircase, so characteristic of the period, still remains, though generally greatly mutilated.

These courtyards—of which there are many at Campden and Northleach—are delightfully picturesque and are reminiscent of similar instances on the Continent, showing how similar treatments of the same subject produce much the same result in effect, even though executed by different people, hundreds of miles apart. One remarkably fine house, the *Old Bear Inn*, standing in the main street, no doubt owes its name to some connection with the great Earl of Warwick, and there are continuous references to this inn in the Burgesses books from the commencement of the seventeenth century. It has a beautiful oriel window in the centre of the street front, and though its architectural composition

FIG. 83. ORIEL WINDOW AT BURFORD.

has been much mutilated, enough remains to show what the building was originally like.

Only a short time ago the staircase, enclosed in a circular turret with a high pointed roof, was standing in the large courtyard at the back, but within the last ten years this has unfortunately been pulled down.

All over Burford are typical examples of Cotswold building, and though few are in their original state, even now they are extremely pleasing, and show by what simple and straightforward means such charming effects were gained. To architects the work is especially interesting, for we can see how the different styles and periods overlapped, how traditions lingered, and how loth the builders were to give up accustomed methods. As is the case in all these Cotswold towns and villages, there are many beautiful Renaissance buildings scattered about the streets of Burford, delightful and pleasing touches of a later date, full of charm and simple dignity, and with exquisite detail.

Campden, like Burford, Northleach, and other Cotswold towns, was the abode of rich wool-merchants, who have left behind them lasting traces of their taste, in fine examples of mediaeval art and of their wealth and piety in the fifteenth century church. It is almost unique amongst the many interesting towns, and within its small limits contains some beautiful examples of domestic architecture.

Here we find all styles, from the exquisitely delicate fourteenth century work in the remains of the old town hall, to the stately and scholarly work of Sir Baptist Hicks and the dignified examples of Queen Anne and the early Georges. Small they may be, and perhaps to the passer-by insignificant and hardly noticeable, but all betraying that sense of fitness of purpose and simplicity of expression so characteristic of English architecture at these periods.

We find in Campden the genuine Cotswold commonsense style of building brought almost to perfection, for it lies in the heart of the stone district, and this material is used almost to the exclusion of all others.

Apart from the picturesqueness of its long street, with the somewhat unusual arrangement of groups of isolated buildings, and the strong and sturdy character of its architecture, it is singular in possessing a series of buildings, designed evidently by one hand and erected within a few years of each other.

Though possessing all the charm and variety of the local work, they are stamped with a scholarly feeling and grasp of design and composition that impart an air of distinction apart from the other buildings in the town, and before dealing with them more in detail, a short account of the causes that led to their erection may not be out of place.

As mentioned before, Campden owed its prosperity to its wool trade in the fourteenth and fifteenth centuries, and reached the zenith of its prosperity during the time when England was the great centre and distributor of finished goods all over Europe.

The town has been continuously mentioned by early chroniclers from the seventh century; its historical interest increasing with succeeding years. A search through the Patent Rolls and records reveals many most interesting facts concerning the lives and doings of its inhabitants during the Middle Ages.

In the church there are a series of memorial brasses and tablets to many eminent "woolmen," as they were styled; amongst others that of William Grevel, citizen of London, "flos mercatorum lanar 'tocuis Anglie," who died in 1401, and his wife Marion in 1386. Part of Grevel's house, built at the close of the fourteenth century, is still standing in the main street, the superb bay window, two storeys in height, so delicately wrought both inside and out, showing the interest and pride that must have been taken in these houses of our forefathers.

After passing through many hands the Manor was bought in 1609 by Sir Baptist Hicks, a wealthy and influential mercer of London, sometime Lord Mayor. He succeeded to his father's business at the sign of the *White Bear* in Cheapside, where he supplied the Court with " silks, satins and rich mercery wares," and in addition made a large fortune through money-lending transactions with the nobility, even extending, so it is said, to the king himself. In 1612 in the height of his prosperity, he bought a large property in Kensington and built himself a town house at Campden Hill, which, after undergoing many vicissitudes, was destroyed by fire in 1862.

In 1613 he commenced to build a large mansion at Campden, on the high ground overlooking the vale to the south of the church, but this also came to the same untimely ending, being unfortunately burnt purposely during the Civil War under the mistaken impression that it would fall into the hands of the Parliamentarians.

Sir Baptist Hicks was raised to the Peerage as Viscount Campden in 1628, and died the following year at another of his London houses in the Old Jewry, and was buried in the South Chapel of Campden Church. He left his two daughters co-heiresses with the enormous fortune (in those days) of £100,000 each. One married Lord Noel, an ancestor of the present Earl Gainsborough, and the other Sir Charles Morison.

When the Civil War broke out the Noels were staunch supporters of the Royalist cause, and Baptist Noel, the third Viscount, raised and kept up at his own expense a regiment of horse and foot soldiers for the service of King Charles I.

It would be out of place here to read this page of history and follow his career, intensely interesting as it is, throughout the Civil War, but after being heavily fined and having much property confiscated by the Parliamentarians, he managed to compound for the estate, and eventually died in 1682 and was buried at Exton in Rutlandshire, another of the family seats, where an enormous monument, the work of Nicholas Stone, was erected to his memory in the church.

In the chapel in Campden Church are the several monuments to the Hicks and Noel families, the largest and most striking being that of Sir Baptist Hicks and his wife. It is very elaborate, of black and white marble, finished with pediments and a canopy supported by twelve columns of Egyptian porphyry. Beneath are effigies both lying in their state robes and coronets upon a black marble slab. There is unfortunately no record of either the designer or sculptor of this splendid piece of workmanship.

The chapel also contains many other monuments in the form of effigies and busts, with quaint inscriptions and gorgeously emblazoned coats of arms, all of about the time of Charles I, and apart from their excellent workmanship as examples of the costume of the period, they are well worth noticing.

Sir Baptist Hicks planned his country house on a scale of lavish magnificence even in those opulent days, and with terraces, gardens, fishponds, and extensive outbuildings, it covered a space of over eight acres in extent. Little of the original house remains, excepting the two pavilions at either end of the great terrace, the entrance gateway and the Almonry (Plate xxxii), but these show the fine quality of the work and its peculiar characteristics.

It is to be regretted that the architect of these buildings is unknown, but it is more than probable that Sir Baptist, being one of the wealthiest men of his day, would have employed a man of recognized skill and ability in his profession.

By the same hand are the Almshouses, (Plate x), a simple group of buildings on a raised terrace, overlooking one of the approaches to the great house, and in the main street the beautiful old Market Hall, dated 1627, (Plate xi), still stands as a testimony to the generosity of Sir Baptist and the skill of his architect.

We may in all probability assign to the same man the rebuilding of the church porch, and the conical tops to the staircase turrets leading to the roofs at the N. and S.W. angle of the nave, also the Jacobean pulpit, brass eagle lectern, and many other details in and about the building.

These few buildings are "foreign" in their origin and conception, in the sense that they were not indigenous to the district. They stand apart from the traditional local work and show traces not only of a more trained hand, but also of the Renaissance feeling which was then prevalent in the centres of learning and culture.

Turning to the Market Hall in the main street, we see that it has five arches on either side, with three gables over them, and a wide solid pier beyond, and two arches and gables again at each end of the building, with a series of stone columns inside supporting the roof trusses. There are windows in the gables, originally glazed, but doubtless blocked up in the days of the window-tax. These are too high, and the labels over them too ill-proportioned for the effect to be pleasing.

There is a decided attempt at a classical composition in the arrangement of the arches supporting the architrave, frieze and cornice, which are carried all round the building, with a parapet above, a gutter behind, and lead gargoyles to throw the water into the street below. At one time there was probably a stone balustrade between the arches overlooking the roadway, but a fragment only now remains. The mouldings and the stone finials are of a character quite different to the traditional work of the country, and a comparison with the building on the other side of the road, (Plate lxi), almost immediately opposite, will better explain the difference than any words can do.

The Almshouses, planned in the form of a letter H with an elongated centre, have precisely similar details with the unusual addition of parapets. The delicate mouldings of the windows, and labels over, vary from those in the district, (Figs. 31–33), the centre mullion of the four-light windows in particular having a circular bead in lieu of the square fillet. The panel containing the coat of arms of the founder both here, and on the Market Hall is the same, (Fig. 84), even to the cutting of the queer little pyramidal ornaments at either corner. The carving to the mantling and crest is done with a vigour and feeling quite beyond that seen in purely local work.

FIG. 84. COAT OF ARMS ON THE MARKET HALL, CHIPPING CAMPDEN.

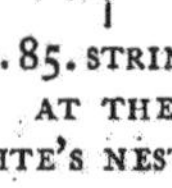

FIG. 85. STRINGS AT THE "KITE'S NEST," CAMPDEN.

The small building, (Pl. xxxii), one of many of those in connection with the great house, shows in its mouldings and general character a close relationship with the other buildings, the string courses being identical and the arrangement of the chimneys with the gable between them, the moulded caps and shafts being the same as those to the almshouses.

Some few miles distant there is a house called the Kite's Nest, which again contains all the peculiarities of detail just referred to, (*see* Fig. 85), and as these are quite unusual in this district, it is perhaps not too hasty a conclusion to draw, that they were all done within a few years of each other and by the same hand.

There are numerous other buildings in Campden which merit more than a passing glance, many of these much later in date, but all containing some detail or characteristic rather out of the common. Look for instance at the house in the main street dated 1705 (Plate ix). This was the period when the fine panelled white rooms of Queen Anne's reign had usurped the place of the low beamed ceilings of the preceding century. We see in the main features of the outward shell the local traditions still adhered to, but the mullioned windows have now a transome and upper lights, though still moulded exactly the same as before. The four-centred doorway is the old form, but instead of the hollow label, we have a delicately moulded cornice and broken pediment showing at a glance the influence, even in these remote parts, of Wren and his school. There is a moulded cornice over the windows and under the eaves of the roof a stone cove. With the exception of these later innovations all else is in the local style, and this house, which is a type of many others scattered about these Cotswold towns, is to architects particularly interesting as showing how the new ideas were grafted on to the older forms.

In the street view, (Plate xcviii), the house in the foreground, which has been much altered in the course of its existence, has a fine gable of somewhat unusual width, not particularly noticeable in itself, except for the arrangement on either side. At the springing of the gable there are two moulded and carved square pedestals, supporting smaller circular vases (*see* Fig. 86). These are in stone, but planted in each is a tulip flower, with leaves and stalks, daintily wrought in iron, a quaint and pleasing conceit which is quite unique in this part of England.

FIG. 86. GABLE AT CAMPDEN.

It is impossible to do more than touch upon the most salient features of these Cotswold houses, but an endeavour has been made to show that in these quiet villages and hamlets work still exists as good and truthful as that which we all so admire in other and more populous parts of the country. We are apt to forget that it is in these villages the history of our country life is written, and that the sturdy yeomen who built these houses and quarried the stone and cut the timber with their own hands, formed a distinct style of architecture.

To-day such buildings are out of the question, for the conditions of life and of labour throughout the whole country are changed, and though this may be a matter for regret, yet it is impossible to revert to the old ways.

But we can gain many valuable lessons from a study of these old buildings, and one is that the necessity of using only the materials to hand contributed greatly to the restfulness of the old work.

There are very few country districts in England that do not possess much beautiful local material, be it stone, or brick, flint or chalk, that is far more suited to its surroundings than strange importations out of harmony with the locality. Modern building suffers because architects do not sufficiently rely upon the use of the materials of the districts they are building in.

Years ago, and to a certain extent even to-day, one could tell by glancing at a building, not only the character of the local materials, but almost the particular district of England in which it was built; each neighbourhood was stamped with its special features, not of style or date, but of material, which in its own particular vernacular, spoke eloquently a language not to be mistaken or confused with that of any other part of the country.

To-day all this delightful tradition seems to be abandoned, and we use all sorts of materials, regardless of their appropriateness, in every part of the country—green Westmorland slates in Kent, red tile hanging in the heart of stone districts, and stone houses in the places where stone is not.

Consequently there is a feeling of unrestfulness pervading

much of the country building of to-day, and it does not seem to fit either its occupants or its surroundings.

In face of the fact that such beautiful work has been done in the past, there is no sound reason for the introduction of "foreign" materials, and to break entirely with the traditional use of local ones, which is now so often done, seems quite unnecessary. Of course it will be urged that expense is the chief obstacle; but the fact that in many parts of England their use has been neglected for so many years, not only adds to the cost, but renders their employment to-day a matter of great difficulty.

Those who build should try to foster and encourage all local crafts and industries, as they are rapidly dying out for want of employment; and it will soon be too late to bring them into use again.

New buildings should be designed in as modern a spirit as we wish, but using the materials at hand. The very fact that in so doing we shall be more or less governed by the same conditions and limitations as these old builders, will give our work to-day a continuity in design and feeling, in harmony with the old, and will help to carry on in a certain sense the spirit and tradition of bygone days, which surely in these times of change and hurry, will appeal to many.

Plate I.

A FARMHOUSE AT STANTON, GLOS.

Plate II.

A FARMHOUSE AT WILLERSEY, GLOS.

Plate III.

COTTAGE WITH PORCH, LITTLE RISSINGTON, GLOS.

Plate IV.

COTTAGES AT STANTON, GLOS.

Plate VI.

COTTAGES AT COLN ST. ALDWYN, GLOS.

Plate VII.

A HOUSE AT WESTON SUBEDGE, GLOS.

Plate VIII.

AT CHALFORD HILL, NEAR STROUD, GLOS.

Plate IX.

HOUSE IN THE HIGH STREET, CAMPDEN, GLOS.

Plate X.

THE ALMSHOUSES, CAMPDEN, GLOS.

Plate XI.

THE MARKET HALL, CAMPDEN, GLOS.

Plate XII.

THE SWAN INN, HARRINGWORTH, NORTHANTS.

Plate XIII.

STREET FRONT OF A FARMHOUSE, LITTLE RISSINGTON, GLOS.

Plate XIV.

BACK OF A FARMHOUSE, LITTLE RISSINGTON, GLOS.

Plate XV.

A FARMHOUSE AT GRETTON, NORTHANTS.

Plate XVI.

COTTAGES AT CHEDWORTH, GLOS.

Plate XVII.

COTTAGES AT FINSTOCK, OXON.

Plate XVIII.

A COTTAGE AT FINSTOCK, OXON.

Plate XIX.

THE POST OFFICE, DUCKLINGTON, OXON.

Plate XX.

COTTAGES AT GRETTON, NORTHANTS.

Plate XXI.

THE MANOR HOUSE, GRETTON, NORTHANTS.

Plate XXII.

A COTTAGE AT BLISWORTH, NORTHANTS.

Plate XXIII.

COTTAGES AT AWKWARD HILL, ARLINGTON, GLOS.

Plate XXIV.

A COTTAGE AT BIBURY, GLOS.

TUDOR HOUSE, MICKLETON, GLOS.

Plate XXVI.

A HOUSE AT SNOWSHILL, GLOS.

Plate XXVII.

VIEW IN THE VILLAGE STREET, BROADWAY, WORC.

Plate XXVIII.

THE VILLAGE CROSS AND A COTTAGE, STANTON, GLOS.

Plate XXIX.

THE GROCER'S SHOP, COLLEY WESTON, NORTHANTS.

Plate XXX.

TOP FARM, BROADWAY, WORC.

Plate XXXI.

TOP FARM, BROADWAY, WORC.

Plate XXXII.

THE "ALMONRY," CAMPDEN, GLOS.

Plate XXXIII.

A COTTAGE AT STANWAY, GLOS.

Plate XXXIV.

A FARMHOUSE AT LAVERTON, NEAR BROADWAY, GLOS.

Plate XXXV.

BACK OF A FARMHOUSE, LAVERTON, NEAR BROADWAY, GLOS.

Plate XXXVI.

A FARMHOUSE AT SAINTBURY, GLOS.

Plate XXXVII.

A STREET VIEW, PAINSWICK, GLOS.

Plate XXXVIII.

HOUSES AT WESTON SUBEDGE, GLOS.

Plate XXXIX.

WARREN HOUSE, STANTON, GLOS.

Plate XL.

DOORWAY AT WARREN HOUSE, STANTON, GLOS.

Plate XLI.

A COTTAGE AT CHALFORD HILL, NEAR STROUD, GLOS.

A COTTAGE AT LILFIELD, NEAR STROUD, GLOS.

Plate XLII.

Plate XLIII.

DOORWAY AT BOWMEADOW FARM, LAVERTON, NEAR BROADWAY, GLOS.

Plate XLIV.

HOUSE IN ST. PAUL'S STREET, STAMFORD, NORTHANTS.

Plate XLV.

IN CHURCH STREET, STROUD, GLOS.

Plate XLVI.

A STREET VIEW AT CIRENCESTER, GLOS.

Plate XLVII.

A SMALL HOUSE AT WITHINGTON, GLOS.

Plate XLVIII.

THE MANOR FARM, RAMSDEN, OXON.

Plate XLIX.

COTTAGES AT WESTON SUBEDGE, GLOS.

Plate L.

THE VILLAGE SCHOOL, ASTON SUBEDGE, GLOS.

Plate LI.

THE VILLAGE SCHOOL, ASTON SUBEDGE, GLOS.

Plate LII.

THE COURT FARM, BROADWAY, WORC.

Plate LIII.

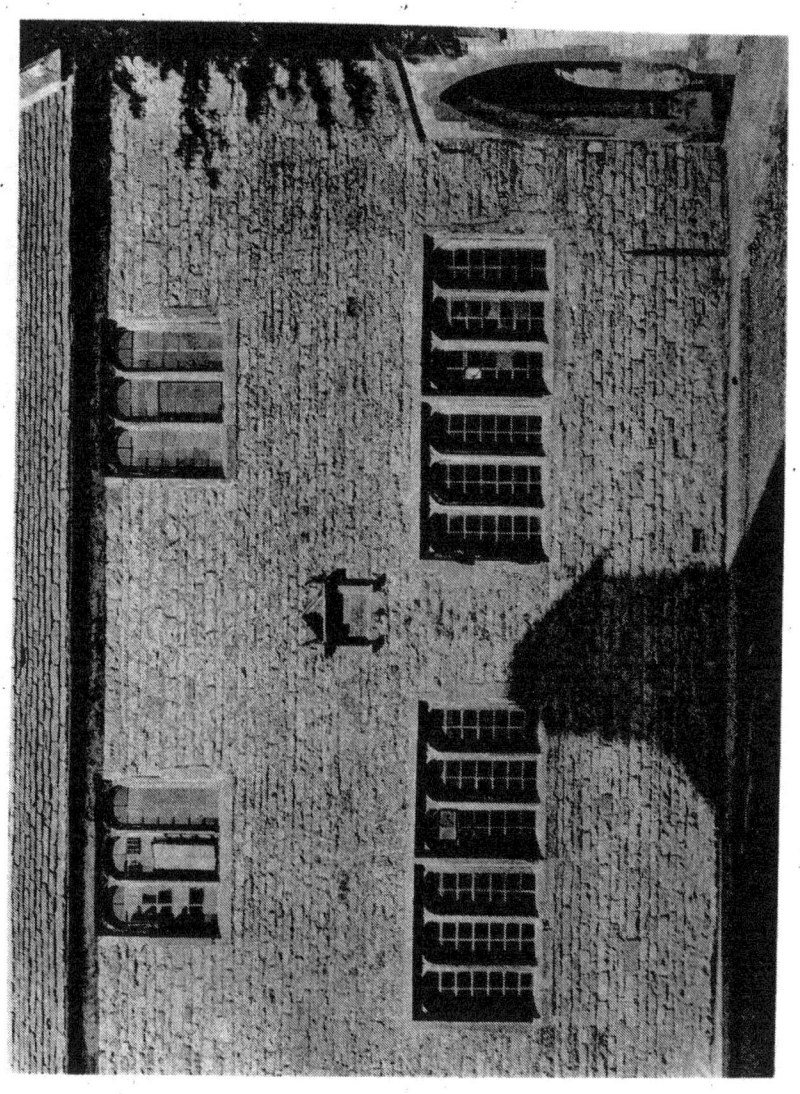

ST. EDWARD'S GRAMMAR SCHOOL, STOW-ON-THE-WOLD, GLOS.

Plate LIV.

THE SOUTH FRONT, MANOR FARM, TEMPLE GUITING, GLOS.

Plate LV.

END OF SOUTH FRONT, MANOR FARM, TEMPLE GUITING, GLOS.

Plate LVI.

THE SCHOOL HOUSE, BAMPTON, OXON.

Plate LVII.

COTTAGES AT YARWELL, NORTHANTS.

Plate LVIII.

A COTTAGE AT DUDDINGTON, NORTHANTS.

Plate LIX.

COTTAGES AT CHIPPING CAMPDEN, GLOS.

Plate LX.

THE SWAN INN, LECHLADE, GLOS.

Plate LXI.

A STREET HOUSE IN CAMPDEN, GLOS.

Plate LXII.

THE PLOUGH INN, CALLOWELL, NEAR STROUD, GLOS.

Plate LXIII.

A FARMHOUSE AT NASSINGTON, NORTHANTS.

Plate LXIV.

A FARMHOUSE AT BARFORD, OXON.

Plate LXV.

A GABLE FROM LYDDINGTON, RUTLAND.

Plate LXVI.

A HOUSE AT BOURTON-ON-THE-WATER, GLOS.

Plate LXVII.

A COTTAGE AT NASSINGTON, NORTHANTS.

Plate LXVIII.

COTTAGES AT WESTON SUBEDGE, GLOS.

Plate LXIX.

A COTTAGE WITH DORMER AT STANTON, GLOS.

Plate LXX.

Plate LXXI.

A GROUP OF COTTAGES, BIBURY, GLOS.

Plate LXXII.

THE MANOR HOUSE, WITHINGTON, GLOS.

Plate LXXIII.

Plate LXXIV.

BACK OF AN INN, NEAR STROUD, GLOS.

Plate LXXV.

DEAN ROW, COLN ST. ALDWYN, GLOS.

Plate LXXVI.

A COTTAGE WINDOW, BROADWAY, WORC.

Plate LXXVII.

THE BAKER'S HOUSE, BOURTON-ON-THE-HILL, GLOS.

Plate LXXVIII.

THE CARPENTER'S SHOP, BOURTON-ON-THE-HILL, GLOS.

Plate LXXIX.

A FARMHOUSE AT PAXFORD, GLOS.

Plate LXXX.

FRONT VIEW OF MEDFORD HOUSE, MICKLETON, GLOS.

Plate LXXXI.

THE ENTRANCE, MEDFORD HOUSE, MICKLETON, GLOS.

Plate LXXXII.

EAST END OF MEDFORD HOUSE, MICKLETON, GLOS.

Plate LXXXIII.

THE KITCHEN CHIMNEY, MEDFORD HOUSE, MICKLETON, GLOS.

Plate LXXXIV.

THE VILLAGE INN, WILLERSEY, GLOS.

Plate LXXXV.

COTTAGES AT EBRINGTON, GLOS.

Plate LXXXVI.

HUMPHRIES END FARM, NEAR STROUD, GLOS.

Plate LXXXVII.

A COTTAGE AT WOODCHESTER, NEAR STROUD, GLOS.

Plate LXXXVIII.

COTTAGES AT LAVERTON, NEAR BROADWAY, GLOS.

Plate LXXXIX.

COTTAGES AT PAINSWICK, GLOS.

Plate XC.

THE RECTORY, COLN ROGER, GLOS.

Plate XCI.

A HOUSE AT CHEDWORTH, GLOS.

THE BULL AND SWAN INN, STAMFORD, NORTHANTS.

THE WHITE LION INN, OUNDLE, NORTHANTS.

Plate XCIV.

CALLOWELL FARM, NEAR STROUD, GLOS.

Plate XCV.

COTTAGES AT CHEDWORTH, GLOS.

Plate XCVI.

Plate XCVII.

THE TOLSEY, HIGH STREET, BURFORD, OXON.

Plate XCVIII.

THE MAIN STREET, CAMPDEN, GLOS.

Plate XCIX.

AT WESTINGTON, NEAR CAMPDEN, GLOS.

Plate C.

A FARMHOUSE AT LEONARD STANLEY, NEAR STROUD, GLOS.

Lightning Source UK Ltd.
Milton Keynes UK
UKHW022258271022
411228UK00003B/78